T0064733

2021
A NEW DAWN

GAYLE SCHILZ

authorHOUSE®

AuthorHouse™ LLC
1663 Liberty Drive
Bloomington, IN 47403
www.authorhouse.com
Phone: 1-800-839-8640

Published by AuthorHouse 09/05/2014

ISBN: 978-1-4772-8791-0 (sc)
ISBN: 978-1-4772-8792-7 (e)

Contents

I hope this book inspires you to open your eyes for the coming of 2021, A New Dawn. It will be a new time. The entire psychic is changing. We must purify our minds, body and soul. We must elevate ourselves to be angelic. This age is going to be awareness, experience and wisdom. Everything comes from our source, that source is god. We are entering the Age of AQUARIUS. It will be the age of knowledge, faith and trust. It will only be for those who keep up. We will become united as one, a new beginning.

With the Age of Aquarius, everything will be different. Our world will be different. Politics, our nation, the land, and the boundaries will be different. Things will happen; changes are inevitable. We are living in a world disrupted by planetary changes. Political wars while things are moving and shifting incredibly fast. We have to be stable to serve others. We have to touch every heart while we are here to make a change in this world. We can change the world through our sustenance, grit commitment, character, dignity, grace and radiance. We have to serve all over the world. We need to serve the global community now as everything is changing. It all comes to pass. The Aquarian age you don't pray. You ask god to pray for you. Tell God," Lord pray for me that I should be as infinite as you. Make me as bright, bountiful and beautiful as you. Lord give me the power of love to serve, let me know to serve myself, let me touch and heal, let my sight create miracles where I exist".

Forgive your environment and people. Always repeat, "I am healthy, I am happy, I am holy". Don't control the world. Control yourself. Drink a cup of joy, it is time to rejoice. Forgive your past, walk in the light, ask your angels to guide you. It is time to immerse yourself, within the self.

We need people like the Gurus, Gandhi the AREC lenic, ECT…to get others on the right track before 2021. Don't change the world change yourself. God will supply you with everything you need. Love inspires and illumines and designates the way. Every day, fill yourself with peace, love, joy, health, and good thoughts. If you want something, don't go get it, let it come to you. If you keep trying, it is beyond reach. Forget who you are. Reach out. Heal the world. When you hear someone else's problems, problems will disappear. Gods and the heavens will be kind to you.

"Awaken Your Own Better Self"

Look in the mirror of your eyes to see yourself as what you really are, so you can face the world and have the strength and spirit and save you from duality and royalty. So you can face the world in peace and tranquility.

ACKNOWLEDGEMENTS

I am dedicating this book to Edgar Cayce. With great respect and love for this great being he was, and still is, coming to me though my dreams, the teachings, the principals, philosophy. I woke up one morning all I could think about was Edgar Cayce to write a book, the thought came to me that we will be guided into the new kingdom. The greatest miracle is unity (for the entire world Edgar Cayce did for others he is still coming through to us from the spirit world.) His work does not end, as he is a great psychic and prophet. I was cured of epilepsy through the Edgar Cayce handbook. One day to I was doing yoga I came up in the cobra, and I felt cleansed, no more epilepsy thanks to Edgar Cayce and God.

One of the apostles of Jesus had epilepsy. After he came out of the spell he could predict the future.

I am truly grateful for a friend of mine who adopted me in her heart, brought me up with Edgar Cayce. She told me she is coming back to me through a trumpet Addie told me many things and wanted me to take over her readings. My experiences are different than hers as she passed away, my deepest gratitude to those who came into my life and are still in my dreams.

I had the greatest parents in the world. Right before my dad passed awake he touched my face and a flash of light came to my head. I feel we are all connected in some way. My mom and I were real close. A few days before she died, moms voice grew faint she was deleting everything she knew from her childhood until she entered the new dawn.

The morning my mom passed awake the nurse said", your mom took her last breath". I stood up and felt this energy go through my body as she was leaving this earth planet. I had a wart on the bottom of my foot for three years. Three different doctors couldn't get rid of it. I looked at my foot the wart was gone. I felt cleansed inside. I never knew what kind of life I would have, with whatever happens, I just keep on going.

Through the Edgar Cayce ARE clinic, with yoga, spiritual healing, staying on a spiritual path, and helping others, we can all make it and to face challenges in life, life that presents us no matter how hard it may seem as we can achieve our dreams. You have to find inner peace and strength within yourself.

Doing yoga over forty-five years, with meditation, hand mudras, therapeutic touch as well. I pray every day for all those concerned. I hope what else you do in life, do it with grace and love. I hope this book will give you a more positive mental attitude to cope with your everyday experiences. May God fill your life with peace and love as he did mine.

Don't change the world. Change yourself.

With Great Respect and Love
Gayle

Aquarius 2021

The Age of Aquarius is coming our way. We have to take away emptiness, insanity and pain for judgment day. We sit in this world. We have to remain disciplines in this undisciplined world. We have to master ourselves. We need character, commitment and grace. We have to overflow with energy touch the hearts and fill this empty space. Our actions will be great. We will create a new human race. We want life to be right for all out children. We want the whole society to find inner peace, to laugh, love and shine because life is only a lease on time and space.

So do your part and live in peace. Yet if this world would disappear from view, still it would be the same.

Did you ever hear, people with experiences shall live, people with knowledge shall die?

Wake up to your own inner self, God dwells in you as you. We are all here for a reason to change ourselves of who we are, and why birds have wings to remind us of our past, in the past and now. How angels saved people, trust God will send his angels again to save us.

CHAPTER 1
PROSPERITY

"Attitude of Gratitude"

Pause for a second when you listen and speak. In one second you can see the light and have total effectiveness than the third eye. Take this second to lift. It is the beaming of your command center. When people talk listen, stop for a second and answer. You will be shocked how much you know. Be grateful you are breathing and alive. So don't go and get it, let it come to you. "Character brings you prosperity".

When people have calamity and misfortune adversity, these three sisters come to visit who react to them. Opportunity, fortune and good luck are the three sisters who come to visit those who are calm, quiet and peaceful. Embrace life live kindness compassion and serve. All of this is knowledge, happiness, prosperity and richness.

Serving is the only way to elevate your consciousness. Doing community service, others doing something where there is no status, no reward. Your reward is hundred- thousand- fold from the heavens. It is called seeding the fortune. God is always willing to give, but are we willing to receive.

When you cannot give you cannot progress. If you are scared, you are very insecure, then you feel terrible and miserable, then you live the rest of your life with a lot of pain. We have so many environments of pressure: weight, value, status and virtues. Then we suffer. The actual fact is we want to suffer. But if you relax, we could never suffer. If you could take 11 min

1

a day every morning it will help you to understand god- that god is the doer of everything. "Let your energy flow".

When you think of your child or his strength tomorrow, think of that child as an angel or yourself. Never recognize your child, you'll never recognize God. Be healthy, Be happy, Be holy... People carry the world in the palm of their hands. Doing Kundalini Yoga is the reserve energy to open the light of god.

We're not here by any accident or incident. We are here to connect and join, or disconnect and lose. The hand of god which created you should carry you and will carry if you let it be. While you grow spiritually then we let everybody grow with us. Our words affect our hearts and bring confusion to clarity, then ill-health, then certain situations in life a place where we can understand how great it is to be healthy. When you lean to a path of individual prosperity and spirituality and your surroundings are rich indeed. We should try to understand each other for we are here on this earth to visit.

People are struggling with their narrowness and shortcomings. They are confined to collect the weather. They are unhappy because someone else has what they want. God is the one who manages and arranges the circumstances which simple therapy can help people.

This is a formula to help cleanse peoples' minds of parasites- which are called thoughts, miserable dirty thoughts. Pondering humans, cleansing ourselves of these parasites can be very difficult. We may have guilt and try to get rid of that guilt but we can't. We forget God is with us all the time. What we need to know is to understand the technology and psychology the way to make a very small little being to a big vast being.

May we all live as a nation and understanding life as we grow in this essence, have peace and power of peace within you. Remember God is with us. May we all live in piety and prosperity?

There is no room for doubt. Faith is an assumption. Faith is the assumption that the universe will take care. It is the assumption which causes the effect, envelope yourself in the gentle, loving, and abundant arms of the universe. Allow yourself to be taken care of. May God bless you that the bounty of the universe belongs to us all. Never doubt. Change your negative thoughts into positive right away. Have faith in yourself and God.

When things go wrong giggle and let go of the anger. You have to have a meditated mind to wait and see what will come to you. Through God, our mind will direct us to work in the right channels and be the right channels, be in the right place at the right time and deliver.

Through God, our mind will direct us to work in the right channels and be in the right place at the right time. We will then experience love, joy and happiness, our spiritual discipline has much to do with how we relate to ourselves and to each other, to understand god in the Aquarian time. How we will accept ourselves and others in a state of grace without needing to control or change the situation; what effect will it have on our social world?

Believe in that which is not, in order that it may be the imagination is the creative power in our hands. Everything in which we have faith, succeed. For 3,000 years, man has been told to find a Guru. For the Age of Aquarius, without Guru there is darkness. The embodiment of the body of the word of god is the Shabad Guru, and something which was explained in a simple language of Guru is, you do not have to fine it, "Guru is". Where the Guru is, there shall be no darkness, the impact by the words will vibrate exactly to the orientation, permutation and combination of the micro-consciousness and psyche which is, and shall always be. There shall be no duality, no disconnecting of the self to go through the cycle of change into finding and questioning ones' self, landing in a lot of tragedies.

Drop the Fear and Learn to Hear

Meditation works in the interlock of your head and heart that blocks your ability to actually listen to another person. Communicate for a better tomorrow, not to spoil today. Saying one wrong word can do much more harm than you could ever imagine, even estimate. Engulf the situation by bringing a smile to it.

With the Age of Aquarius we should not fight about how we should worship God, since there is one God who breathes in all of us. You should clean your bodies and your minds, go out and earn a living, righteously, and share with others who are less fortunate. The human race is about to go berserk. If you are not looking for peace you are the peace, you create the peace, you are the part of the peace. When good comes we should share it, when bad comes we excel it.

Three things in life- peace of mind, peace of a nation and peace of the world, if the mind is not at peace it does not have harmony. It cannot win the war of challenge. A person may look beautiful, buy the whole world with money, but that person shall be unfulfilled, empty and unhappy.

Many people have taken up yoga to help relieve stress, cope with anger and build self-esteem.

Soon we will actually enter the Aquarian Age. We have seen the world through the turmoil and it is not over yet. Drastic changes are happening everywhere, "nothing can remain hidden". As the new age enters a lot more is bound to surface." Infinity has everything, when you relate to infinity, Infinity gives you everything". When you give a lot of things, we give for the sake of giving. We give for the sake of a better relationship. It is second nature to give. Maybe we have not learned to give unconditionally. The only person who can give unconditionally is one (who feels that comes from God).

To quit is to let go, to let go is to open up; to open up is to receive. When you pray for your children and see things wrong, don't give them any energy. When you face tragedy, apply spiritual strength. It takes one thought to make a friend. One Guru said the animosity against the united Stated is that America is under attack. This is the first time in the world civilians have been attacked this way, and it took just a handful of people to put their life at stake to do this. The Guru said it is true we have a collective responsibility, we are one, we will also suffer as one and we will act as one. All these people who died had not even a thought, this only thought. Their only crime was that they were Americans. Understand this was a well- planned attack.

You figure it out that when I'm crying that the Age of Aquarius is coming, this is a period of insanity beforehand. Do you believe it? See what has happened, and now more things are expected. It is a tragedy we have to face. Tomorrow when they count everything it will be a bigger tragedy than it is today. We offer our prayers- in silence, our heads bowed to the Almighty seeking His protection, compassion for those left behind, healing energy for those who are injured. Pray from our hearts to God Almighty, under Gods protection, we are always open to danger. As in WW II, Japan attacked Pearl Harbor, we could have pocketed it, but we didn't. Guru said, it's of every American to keep on pocketing a lot of things until it goes over the line, than we won't pocket it anymore. That is the way America will go. Pearl Harbor brought WW II and made us participate. Out whole lifestyle changed. We weren't the same again and we are not going to be the same ever. This is what religion is all about. Search your inside give yourself a chance eliminate your fantasies and your imagination. Don't live in a dream world. Things can happen and that is what happened. The enemies plan all the time. You have to defend a thousand times; the enemy wants one chance, which they got when the World Trade Center was attacked. Now it is upon the nation to respond, these kinds of things will be repeated. Now is the time the concept, which was given to saints and soldiers, comes in handy. We have to be a soldier for the insanity and a saint for this kind of insanity. You have to defend yourself in a saintly, firm way. We have to have spiritual strength. "Applied spiritual strength", is on us. We have to relate both to our inner and outer strength." America will act with one voice, with one determination, and with one strength which is huge."

"We owe our thoughts to the land we live in".

In these tumultuous times, always check with your health practitioner before making any changes to your dietary and exercise programs. A lot of water, fresh juice, if possible, cucumbers and celery for the nervous system watermelon to cool the liver. If you are angry, carrot is a great anti-oxidant. Focus on eating more greens, fresh fruits and vegetables, and whole grains. Avoid processed foods are refined sugar. Supplements: a good multivitamin, vitamin A, C, E and selenium, an essential fatty acid, a good B vitamin, when the body is stressed, healing acupuncture, chiropractic and massage to keep the energy flowing smoothly. Long deep breathing can calm and relax the body. Left nostril breathing can calm the mind. Yoga can strengthen the nervous system to give you energy and strength. Meditation helps subconscious minds process life's events to heal others and to relax.

Did you know that there are 108 elements in this Universe which are at the tip of your finger, provided you decide to be compassionate, kind and caring, you expand in kindness prosperity comes with it. No matter whom we write about we are one and will soon be together. This is why we are here. We are supposed to serve, help, liberate, share with others and God will share with us. All we need is to forget who we are and help another person. Reach out, this is the life. We are on this planet to serve people.

Have you heard yourself say, "I have no time", "in time to come" and" in the past"? These thoughts are what keep us from experiencing the moment. There is nothing more important than bringing your full attention into what you are doing right now. We have to watch our thoughts by learning to control our thoughts when we enable ourselves to control our lives. Having freedom in our thoughts frees us in every facet of our lives. Our thoughts become feelings, our feelings become our emotions. Then our emotions become our desires and desires overtake to the point of utter misery. Don't reach your desired goals or objects.

Different meditations and help you to succeed in anything you want to be, after all, it is just a thought. A MANTRA is like a telephone. God is like a first responder. There are a lot of lines in God's house. If he doesn't answer, leave a message. Call on God- the entire world will call on?

The ideal that a disciplined spiritual practice brings health, humility and wisdom, The Aquarian times will show us a whole new view of prosperity. Fear, you have not seen the light inspire each other. We are all together in the consciousness of the one creator. Impress the whole world can serve anyone. We'll have the whole world in the palm of your hand, no limit to what you can do.

Forget the past. Walk in the light.

CHAPTER 2
TRANSFORMATION AWAKEN

Transformation; awaken to your destiny- connect with your soul to connect with the infinite. Fall in love with the experience of your soul. Singing is so good for the soul. With yoga, meditation and chanting, all these can lift you from depression, insecurity, nightmares and loss, imparts patience and stability, self-esteem into complete self-confidence. When you feel a sense of failure within the self, grant grace and will show you the way to find your path in life. Brings freedom and liberation, gives knowledge, brings with meditation, changing inner silence helps to remove the veil of illusion. The technology of yoga and the secrets of the body, if you listen, pain and sin are erased. Dive deep into the ocean of virtue, only one who has faith comes to know such a state of mind.

The faithful know all about all worlds and realms. The path of the faithful shall never be blocked. The faithful shall depart with honor and fame.

When your body and feet are dirty, you can wash it away. But when the intellect is polluted by sin, actions repeated over and over are engraved in the soul. You shall harvest what you plant. Let your spiritual wisdom be your food and compassion your attendant.

Having created the creation the Creator Lord watches over it. Remember by their deeds and their actions they shall be judged. The good and the bad shall be judged.

CHAPTER 3
REFLECTIONS

Evil uses a person, people are victims of evil. You give evil the power to hurt you. What you see in others is a reflection of you! There are no limitations to the imagination. Don't change the world, change yourself. Snap out of the way you feel. You should have a strong determination to succeed.

You will pass this way only once so if you can do good for anyone do it now. Call on your loved ones in the spirit world. They are waiting to hear from you and bless you. They are just beyond the physical world. Arise. Awake your own inner self. Lighten up, don't worry. Drink a cup of joy.

When you love your enemies, God will surely come looking for you. God holds the mystery of life and death. That authority over your illness, the truth makes all things possible. Invite gods will to become your will. Why worry? Why fear? The Lord of the universe is watching over you. Knowledge is the true giver of light. We must trust Gods will to become our will. Relax. Let the tension in you flow like water right out of your body

Bow to your heart and thank it
Love people for who they are, not what they are.
Your body is a temple and it goes with us always.
Because the power of illusion we are not able to experience our true self.
Let go of the self through meditation and selfless service.

Know god to know the truth, to experience love unconditionally. When we become quiet in every sense of the word we get rid of thoughts we do not need to have. The self will shine forth. When you are silent and at peace actions happen for you and for the benefits of the world. Always respect the self. Until that there is respect of the self, it does not matter how many churches we visit, temples, there is no real peace. But when we respect the self, then we can attain true happiness and our contentment.

A spiritual path is worship and respect, not just a set of riches if it is done with nothing but love. The self is everywhere and in everything. You don't have to give up things you can find God right where you are. Take a broom and sweep your heart clean. Give up your ego. It is the self. Pursue this awareness. I am the self. Keep worshiping your own self cause God dwells within you as you.

Poor indeed is he who does not ever show anger but worse indeed is he who cannot control it in himself. They must fail. Though often those who flare up quickly also forgive quickly if they remain a little children asking, seeking, living," guide thou me, O God in the steps I take and in the words I say day by day". God exists in all people he is present in every heart. You don't have to do anything to look for him.

Doubt is your worst enemy. "When you give up your doubts, knowledge spontaneously arises from within". Have faith. Whatever you practice, that is what becomes, you. "Inner wealth comes from within, and then your world will turn into nectar". Only through the power of faith you become free everywhere in this world. No more obstacles will hold you hostage.

Put aside gossip. Chant God's name. By using your energy, inhale this energy. It is right within you, lives in you and your heart. You are a true house of God. "There is no place or no person where God does not exit."

Once you know what is good for you or what is harmful, you must choose for yourself what is beneficial. When we celebrate a great being, greatness manifests in our own being. Let your greatness be expressed towards others. Know the truth and the truth will set you free. Whatever related to yesterday will take away the energy you need to handle tomorrow. We have the freedom to choose the experience of bondage of worldly life experience, the truth of our existence.

Just look in the mirror of your heart. You will know what you are. Give yourself some time every day; it will take away the rough edges. That light will reveal itself through you. For a new enriched and happy life talk to your higher self.

CHAPTER 4
"The Self"

The vibrations of the whole world pass through your body because there is a constant exchange between you and your surroundings and the people who come in contact. But to receive magnetism, you must be near the Lord of the divine.

Hypnotism has been called animal magnetism; it's a sort of mental chloroform through the suggestion of the hypnotist. Spiritual magnetism is something else. It is the power of the soul to attract or create whatever needs for happiness and wellbeing. Sometimes I think the body is like a computer. It is how you use it. We are all connected in some way, and we will all meet again.

Fasting cleanses your blood, gives rest to the organs, and revitalizes energy through your lips and hands and feet. You can transmit healing energy to others when praying. When you are weak you will receive others vibrations. Shun the company of those with bad habits. Only the strong minded can mingle with such people without being.

Mans' life is cut of years of his life with the noisy vibrations and noise. Vibrations of all kinds affect the nervous system. If you become calm and strong in your mind it cannot touch you. Think, "I am happy" every day. Affirm that thought. You will develop your own magnetism to change yourself for the better. Always keep your body and soul clean and neat. Mix only with people you want to be. You can steal magnetism from the saints, other people thousands of miles away. Spiritual vibrations are limitless. Offer prayers in silence with our head bowed to the Almighty seeking His protection, kindness and compassion for those left behind, seeking the healing energy for those who are injured. Let us pray from our hearts to God Almighty. If a person speaks with only his soul, people will want to listen. You can change others with just your words. This is magnetism. Everything is a state of mind. You can make yourself happy or unhappy. You can feel that person is living this world. My mom and I were at a club I go to. We were sitting and watching people dance, after the music stopped, this couple was leaving the floor and I told my mom that man is going to die shortly. I heard two weeks later he was outside with his wife in the garden and he did not feel well he went in the house and lay on the bed two hours later he died, this was two weeks later. It is just at times I am in tune with the universe. When I go shopping I glance at those books on the way out and I said something is going to happen to that movie star, two weeks later on the news they broke up.

It is sad to see the prejudice in the hearts of people in all religions today, be loyal to your spiritual path. All paths lead to God. Through self-control you will attain self-mastery and real happiness. Your thoughts can uplift you or degrade you. You are the master of moments of your life. Use this wisely, always have right thoughts, don't be with people who smoke. It will be a waste of life and the most vicious thing you can do for your soul. It would be better if you took a walk and get some healthful exercise.

The words that come out of the cannon of the mouth have the power to explode empires. We need to do something good everyday instead of wasting time on things. Each day do something worthwhile. This will make your life more meaningful. Watch your thinking and all your experiences because they can percolate through all your words and actions.

Be careful who your friends are. They reflect you and you reflect them. You have to control your senses or your senses will control you. I'm sure many people felt this vibration but did not know how to act on it. The sooner you dump unhealthy thoughts, the faster healing will come!

One night I was meditating on my friend whom I did not hear from for about 4 years. When I got done meditating, within seconds my phone rang and it was my friend. It is not fair to expect or demand the ultimate perfection from another human being. We ourselves are not perfect. "We should not expect anything from others, but much from ourselves."

Like a marriage, two people that expect nothing from the other, but much of themselves. Marriage should be based on giving. It is sad to see the way marriage is today. I once read that forty thousand couples, husbands and wife, talked to each other on an average of 27 minutes a week. Talk to each other- don't assume that you spouse can guess what is on your mind. That is why god gave us a mouth. Don't take for granted that a spouse knows of your love. Express that affection.

Wisdom and prayer. When people pray, at times their minds are focused on food and going out or other stray thoughts. If you keep on praying in spite of mental wandering those thoughts will eventually die down. You will feel god in your life, you will be happy. What your soul has lost from the time of Adam and Eve is the joy that is God. Talent is nothing but one hundred percent attention applied in some previous life that is what genius is.

Communion with God in daily meditation, and prayer are our greatest weapons against disease, sorrow, misunderstanding, and other forms of discord. Keep God's presence within you always. The kind of food you eat has a great effect on your development of a good or bad disposition. Let your food be your medicine; let your medicine be your food. If you make good and healthy choices, you will have more freedom and power than ever before. If you become in tuned with God you will experience peace and joy. If God is for you, who can be against you?

Harmony is a fact. This world is only a dream. Use your divine mind. Your mind is the source of all movement. Power of thought can meet your needs anywhere. Some people have no control over themselves it is a lack of weakness, discipline and power in choosing the positive. It is God's love that loves man, not man's love. Turn your past and future over to God. When you search for love, I will always love you. Don't wait for someone to hug you, hug yourself three times a day. Anything that is related to yesterday is only a memory; don't waste your energy on yesterday it will take away the energy you need to handle tomorrow.

Food is only ordinary matter but it carries the feeling of the people who made it and served it. Don't waste time on others mistakes, don't use God as an excuse for your mistakes. You know your path in life is free; just don't separate yourself from God. Fill all your channels with truth and love. You are the loved of love, with the power of thought you can heal anyone thousands of miles away. Human pity causes pain and suffering. Angel thoughts are God's thoughts passing to man. Don't be conformed to this world; but transformed.

Have only light thoughts, clear the mind. Believe all things are possible, great fears will disappear. Love people for who they are, not what they are. Let everything unfold like a flower and see the beauty in your life. If anything happens to you just say I am better from this mistake. Remember, it isn't what you it, it is what you eat mentally. Take charge of your life and your thought and you can do anything. We have eyes and ears, but sometimes we don't see and sometimes we don't hear. Don't lower yourself to anyone else's level. Healing is a lack of forgiveness, (don't talk about something so it does not materialize). Don't wait for someone to love you, love yourself (repeat love when a negative thought comes up). Every lie is a lack of faith. You create your own destiny. Time is the absolute merge into the absolute. Pour peace and love into yourself.

You are a reflection of what you see spiritually, (look in the mirror you are supreme). Failure is just a stepping-stone toward future success. Don't have faith in matter. Don't look at the things that are seen, but unseen. The things that are seen are temporary, but the things that are unseen are eternal. Dismiss your illness. As soon as you dump unhealthy thoughts, the faster healing can come! Stay on a spiritual path. "Know thy self". Tap into your infinite source of energy and psyche. Forgive yourself and you can do anything. Don't be enslaved, don't be a prisoner in your own body. If you're looking for a mate there is a right time, a right place, a right person. What blesses one blesses all. Listen rather than talk.

1. Watch your thoughts, they become your words.
2. Watch your words, they become your actions.
3. Watch your actions, they become your habits.
4. Watch your habits, they become your character.
5. Watch your character, it becomes your life.

At the end of the day ask your angels to guide you. Always remain in control and calm, let the universe come on and let everything else go. This is the present, the past is dead and the future will take care of itself. Don't be afraid to ask God. If you want perfection win the grace of your mind, keep it calm and serene. If you want freedom, if you want perfection, win the grace of your mind. You have enough love in your heart to fill this entire universe.

If you are with someone and you break up, remember together you expressed God's goodness and likeness and now it is gone. It came from God and is still with you both. It came from your consciousness what you felt was your own completeness it doesn't take another person to make your life that way. You are complete.

A person should be in a position to hold his values clearly in his consciousness. The price of God is living without doubt. So don't doubt, trust God. Get rid of the ego so nothing can destroy you. If you want perfection win the grace of your mind. Keep it calm and serene. If you want freedom, if you want perfection win the grace of your mind. You have enough love to fill this entire universe.

Don't wait for someone to thank. Thank yourself. A person should be in a position to hold his values clearly in his consciousness. The price of god is living without doubt. Get rid of your ego so nothing can destroy you. When you meditate empty yourself and let the universe come into you.

The secret of the soul is awareness. There is so much tension in life that we miss opportunities that come our way. You intuition can be our best friend. When you are in trouble, close our eyes and think. That will be the best thing to do. The purpose of life is to do something that will last forever.

In the Age of Aquarius if you don't have the technical knowledge of the self it will destroy you. If you speak wrong words it will haunt you until death. As you think so you are. Everyone is precious. Even the most rotten person is a creation of God. For every loss there is a gain, for every gain there is a loss.

If you are insecure, bad things will happen. If you don't feel insecure, they will go away. Experience yourself and everything inside you so you won't be a victim of your own permanent fear. Our life is very sacred. Everything is within you; attitude, gratitude and happiness will come to you and go where you go. There is nothing in life more worthy, more beautiful than you. We live by the breath. We were born by the breath and when you die the breath leaves you. Communication, speak through music. No one should control anyone. You should come together like a river and end up in the same ocean.

Live wise and divinely so we don't have to live in any duality. People imprison themselves to sex, food and their way of life. Some people are more afraid of the truth than of life. Never try to solve a fear- drop a fear. Take to the highest part of you and drop them. When you do, you will have people in the palm of your hand. If you love great you become great. If you love small, you become small. Life is a flow of love. Wisdom is telling the truth. When you have pain of fear, you have to forgive yourself. We should be a lighthouse to serve people and light the way.

Meditation can calm the mind and develop your intuition to recognize what is real and important to you. The injury of the tongue is far deeper than the cu of a sword. We meditate to keep our minds sharp and alert, chanting mantras to our souls so we can walk in the light. When you have a problem meditate and face it. The problem in this world is stress. Make your mind a servant, not a master. The best theory is to record your voice and then listen to it, when you bless everyone than you will be blessed.

When you eat, or where you eat, has a direct influence on your mind body and spiritual awareness. Your physical body is a temple; take care of it. If you are not spiritually strong you can't negotiate properly. If you are not mentally strong, you don't have the grit to negotiate. Then we build more guns and bombs. Bring out the inner best. That is the secret of success. Some people are born out of an inferior complex. Keep your body strong so you can do anything. The imagination is the creative power in our hands. No matter how things go, always keep your cool. With the Age of Aquarius it will be a new time. You should purify your mind, body and soul. (This age will serve us of our awareness and experience.)

Believe all things are possible. (It is your strength, pride and soul.) If you don't want to deal with it, then call it impossible. (If it is impossible for God, it is possible for man.) Yoga is a science. It is the purest act by which to live. If you discipline yourself you will know who you are.

When the Muslims conquered India, they destroyed the literature of yoga. They feared the capacity of yoga to make people unconquerable. Talk to your problems. (The thing we can do is restore peace in this turbulent time, have peace within ourselves.) Whatever happened to grateful and hopeful? Take time throughout the day- take a minute to be yourself, love yourself, feel divine. Take a minute to be still and peace within yourself and with everyone. If we stop judging ourselves and others we would be living in paradise. Take control of your life so you can deal with everything with love and kindness.

Knowledge is not outside, it comes from within you. If you direct it, it will become the knower of all. (So if you direct it otherwise, you will become very miserable.) If anyone slanders you or depresses you give them to God. When you speak from the heart you can rule. But, when you speak from the head you destroy. (Don't limit your fear, then you will have unlimited power of inspiration.) Whatever we say lives forever. A wrong word can change our image. Always know you are part of the Universe and the Universe is part of you.

If you can elevate others then you have power. Life is a balance to give you experience and let you discover you within you. Remember we are always being tested. You must find your own depth and test it. You are a "hu-man being". "HU" means spirit, the light, "MAN" means the mental. You are the spirit of your mind. You are the bright light of yourself.

Some people think being religious is about what you believe. Your spirit is the hub. "I am one I am", don't factor your dignity or personality, when you achieve that, all wealth comes to you. Bless yourself. Honor your grace, that God will guide you and give you strength to serve and bring peace. You can be a slave to your way of life. Some people are afraid of the truth than life. We confine ourselves. No one can put you in prison except yourself. Happiness and honesty comes from honest living, we are all born to relate to the future; to silence it will speak to you. The radiance that will give you absolute selflessness, if you make yourself happy when people look at you they will be happy too.

Being old you need wisdom and grace. You will always be rich if you are wise. A lie is a loss of faith. We forget who we are. We are one with God and we should inspire others. Your personality has no power but your performance does. When you bless your enemies and reach out to love the source and cause of calamity, God is with you.

If you get depressed take a cold shower, massage yourself with a towel. Start with the feet until your body turns red. Your thoughts will go away. Isolation is your own fear. We are on a journey going through a planetary shift. A coin has two sides. If you get angry, mad or emotional turn it over and look at the other side. When people are obnoxious they can't change; their behavior is self-damaging. Spirituality is not a religion it is facing yourself with a smile when life confronts you. Remember yourself. God rotates this earth. God will take care of your routine.

People suffer because of impure food and impure thoughts and deeds. Live and let live. Just keep on going. If you don't get anywhere in life it is because you limit yourself. You are the master of your destiny. The Age of Aquarius is upon us. It is the age of peace, tranquility, dignity, grace, and sharing. Soon we will be united. May god bless all of us and all creatures just follow the path of wisdom of your mind. When all rivers come together as one- in the Aquarian Age, we will come together to be one. When you act like God then everything will come to you. Start to meditate and clear your mind so you can face the challenges and pressure. When you follow the grace of your mind, you will win. We are not bound to this world. We have freedom.

CHAPTER 5
QUOTES

Today is today – because tomorrow is not.

1. Temperance-Eat not to dullness drink not to elevation.
2. Silence- Speak not what may benefit others
3. Order- All things have their place.
4. Resolution- Resolve to perform what you ought; perform without fail what you resolve.
5. Sincerity- Use no hurtful deceit, think innocently.
6. Justice- Wrong no one by causing injuries, or omitting the benefit that you are.
7. Moderation- Avoid extremes, forebear resenting life's hurts.
8. Cleanliness- Tolerate no uncleanliness in body, mind and spirit or habitation.

Concentrate on one principle for an entire week, every day of the week. Respond by proper action every time an occasion arises. The second week let your subconscious mind take over. He who cannot forgive, destroys that bridge over which some day he may need to pass. The man of real capabilities, the higher thinker the educated man has no time to spend digging up old skeletons from the closet. Whatever any man did in the past, he himself is accountable to God. It is written down in all its naked truth in his consciousness.

If a spider catches a fly in the web and that fly is strong enough to breath, that enables and escapes, he is a free fly. Prana means energy. Breathing quiets the mind physical, mental and spiritual levels. It is not what you get out of life that counts; it is what you put in the life that counts. Look fear in the mirror, it reflects you just like a candle reflect. Have no fear. "I am the master of myself." Auto suggestion; use your imagination every day in every respect.

I am getting better and better. Say it twenty times in the morning and evening. Repeat my life is better and beautiful. If you are troubled say "NO" it does not trouble me at all, not in the least. Every idea is true and transforms itself into action. God is with me; God is for me, so who can be against me. By letting go it all gets done, the world is won by those who let go. But when you try and try, it is even beyond the winning.

It isn't what you get out of life that counts; it is what you put into life that counts. As a man soweth so shall he reap, as an attitude is held towards another that is gradually built within self. Hence the urge, as it were, to hold what would be called malice, ever determining within the self. ("I'll get even with you yet'" doesn't pay, for this only builds into self that held in thought miracles.) Find less fault with others and they will find fewer faults with you. The way you look at others reflects too small degree the way you truly view yourself in the inner levels of consciousness. There is a lot of power through people. Remember opportunity never stops knocking. Each night burns the records of the day; at sunrise every soul is born again.

Look at one thing to see another to understand what you see is a third, but what you understand is still something else. But to act on what you learn is all that really matters. You make people think they're thinking. They love you but if you really make them think, they hate you! The way we think is the way we live.

Remember we picked this life so we have to live it out. If you don't like your life only you have to change it. Watch your thoughts the way you think is no limit to how much we can learn, it is never too late. If we will only acquire that most important single piece of knowledge that is the knowledge of how little we really know. You have a mind to use. It's never too late. Call on your higher self. "Our mind is our only weapon." You have the greatest level of all things; you have to control your thoughts so they don't control you.

However things go, in life you must remain calm, quiet and peaceful: this peace is the source of prosperity. Self-containment – this is the act of prosperity it is the highest spiritual strength. Nothing can match it. There is an ocean of love within all of us. It is the love of God. It is so pure; it is unconditional. Just let yourself drink this love. God is fully present within us.

If you made a simple effort you can experience God. Let this understanding take you higher and higher. Let this make you feel more and more divine, always trust yourself. Think your trouble is going away? Just as you think you can't open your hands, you have to address yourself to the imagination, not the will. While wiping your hand over your forehead, say it is going away; it is going away 20 to 30 seconds. It should work if you keep repeating it. When you enter a home think of peace in that home, peace in yourself and think of that person being healed. Opportunity never stops knocking. Every night burn the records of the day. At sunrise every soul is born again.

"Auto Suggestion"

Positive; you can do it. Negative; you can't do it. You will feel active full of life- cheerful fit.

"Self-Mastery"

Our actions spring not from our will but from imagination, the influence of the imagination upon the moral and physical being of mankind. Of course the thing must be win our power. Every thought entirely filling our mind becomes true for us and tends to transform itself into action. Say every day in every way, I am getting better and better. You are what you think. All that we think comes true for us. We must not allow ourselves to think wrongly. Nothing in life is to be feared; it is only to be understood.

"Call Death"

1. You call it death, this seemingly endless sleep. We call it birth, the soul , at last, set free.
2. It's hampered not by time or space. You weep, why weep at death. Its immortality.

In the shower sing some kind of Lord 's Prayer, sit or stand in any position and wear white clothes for fifteen minutes, if your depressed, for a half hour. Some people are better at making mistakes than making decisions. (People who don't find time for recreation, sooner or later they will find time for illness)" The might be's and what will happen, they should not concern you now." Action may not bring happiness; but there is no happiness without action. STOP procrastinating. You will gain more weight. It is not the place or condition but you alone can make someone happy or miserable. "You may have many troubles in your life but I bet they never came." What you do is only required of you, you are a slave. The moment you do more, you are a free man.

Think of your life as more of a stepping stone toward a more positive life and attitude, Take off your blinders so you can see the world. Boredom will make you old before your time. Remember the person who lives by himself or for himself is apt to be corrupted by his own company he keeps. You do a lot more by smiling instead of frowning. Your face isn't glass. It won't crack. Learn to laugh at life, life is too short to hold anger, fear the past and now. When you pray, "please" pray for the world and all those concerned. It will make you feel better as a human being. You worry about everything but the outcome may never materialize. Like some people get indigestion before they eat. Know your fear, get rid of it. If you take care of the present, the future will take care of itself. Since man has free will, he is responsible for his actions.

Reason is useless, man should turn to faith. Don't worry about tomorrow; you will have less time to enjoy today. We only pass through this world but once so don't open your umbrella while the sun is still shining. If you keep your good deeds secret, blessings and rewards will be showered upon you.

It is mind over matter when you say you can't do it, but most of the time you can. Use your subconscious mind for a few months to achieve things. Train your body. Recharge your body with play, rest and sleep. You will have better health, positive thoughts and attitudes. Always have something to live for. When you have something to live for, the subconscious mind forces upon the conscious minds strong motivating factors to keep you alive. Remember that the things that are seen for the things that are transient, but the things that are unseen are eternal.

The price of ignorance is sin, sickness and death. Some influences may be mental figments of the imagination. Knowledge is power if only put to use. Thinking good positive and cheerful thoughts will improve the way you feel. What affects your mind affects your body. Develop a positive mental attitude.

I Feel Healthy

I Feel Happy

I Feel Terrific

Enjoy a good life and live longer with a positive mental attitude. Be happy. Great things are in store for you. Have the inner urge to do something. Remember, don't take anything for granted. Faith without words is dead. Direct your thoughts; control your emotions and ordain your destiny. Some people go the extra mile, some have accurate thinking. You should have self-discipline, a pleasing personality, enthusiasm, creative vision, budgeting your time and money, teamwork. Keep your mind positive. If your mind is right, your words will be right. There will never be another like you.

Change your world, and you can achieve anything worthwhile in your life; use your positive mental attitude. It can change your world. Have hope in yourself and others. Having confidence in children will give them confidence in themselves. Set your goals. Write them down. Set a deadline. Set your standards high. Achieve your goals. People are happy as the make up their minds to be. Happiness is a state of mind.

Living with someone, their energy levels and capacities may not be the same as yours. You may not think alike, but attract and repel through verbal communication. (You Are What You Think.) A positive mental attitude can attract you to all the health, wealth and happiness you desire.

If a man is right his words will be right. If you share unhappiness and misery you will attract unhappiness and misery. Be careful who your friends are. They reflect you and you reflect them. What you think you are. If you want something in life you should work for it. If you have a guilty feeling, it's good; but get rid of it. Awaken the sleeping giant within you. There is a devil there is no doubt. Is he trying to get in us or trying to get out? Man has forgotten his God. Man thinks too much of himself.

You only have to answer to one person and that person is God. Failure comes from within. We are never alone; we have our loved ones in the spirit world. Wisdom is the ability to benefit from someone else's experiences. Someone hurts you, forgive them in your heart and you will be free and happy and you will continue and be able to have a better life.

Always thank God if life is good or bad. Everything in life is possible; you will always have miracles happen to you. Every time you lie to a friend it's another shovel of dirt on your grave. (Highest mental power of a man willing to cope with a condition that is infinitely beyond his control and he faces it with the belief that he is going to come through it.)Eating when, how and where direct influence on your mind, body and spiritual awareness. Forgive the past. Walk in the light.

Nobody can control anybody. All you can do is flow with each other like the rivers and streams flow together and end up in the same ocean. To get rid of fear or pain you have to have guts! To forgive yourself, just forgive yourself. When body receives healing from you, this is the best healing. (If you are depressed, moody, angry and rude, empty, what is inside should be stronger than what us outside.) Don't go through life with blinders on. Sometimes we throw the mental influences on the wrong side, hurting those we mean to bless. If God is for us, who can be against us?

Direct your thoughts; control your emotions to ordain your destiny. Through action you get things done. Open your heart to the universe of love and you will be filled.

Who are we? We are the product of life, our environment, physical body, conscious and subconscious mind, experience and heredity. Have always the courage to face the truth. Satisfaction is a mental attitude. Defeat can be a stepping-stone or a stumbling block. If you can spend the time on doing something you won't have much time for accomplishing them. If you keep dwelling on the past and your misfortunes, the greater the power will hurt you. The greatest mistake of all is if you do nothing. The purpose of life is to live your life. Success is a state of mind. If nothing works out, let it go.

When you give things you will have more freedom and power and passions than ever before. The past is done; the future will take care of itself. Know that life is full of limitations but just the opposite. There are endless opportunities, just a matter of listening and moving ahead. Half of your life burden will go away if you just forgive your earthly parents. Just remember, they are good and they did their best. Life is just a lease on time and space, you can secure your tomorrow you can elevate yourself. Now be grateful so your confidence in yourself and your reputation can travel before you.

Dance away stress and fears. If you're uptight you will be dead by tonight. Eating when, how and where direct influence on your mind, body and spiritual awareness. Take one minute to breathe in love, one minute to feel divine and one minute to feel peace with everyone. A person should forgive themselves first before giving advice to someone else.

We value old coins, cheese and wine, yet we do not value old people. They lose their hearing; no one wants to talk to them anymore. They seem to tune out the world around them. Remember when a man of brass or iron guards the state, it will be destroyed. (Petition is the question. Meditation is the answer.) Remember every day in every way you are getting better and better through a positive mental attitude.

No more energy is consumed in using your brain that is just keeping it alive. Don't be afraid to use it. Think with your mind, not your emotions. Sometimes it is easier to believe a lie that has been heard a thousand times than to believe a fact that has never been heard before, If you want to get rid of a problem, write it on a piece of paper and burn it. If you ask a question you may be a fool for five minutes. If you don't ask a question, you remain a fool for life. If you want something done give it to a man who is busy. He'll find time for it.

Just look ahead, at least until tomorrow, as we are each an entity in ourselves. Don't be so hard on yourself. Speaking from experience, I myself have been through more than you will ever know or go through what I did. Laugh at life, know your fears, and get rid of them. What happened a few minutes ago will never happen again. Don't drag the past within you, it is only dead weight, get rid of it and you will feel like you lost weight and you really might lose a few pounds. Your attitude will and the world in your life will get better. Don't hang on to the past. Your future is bright ahead. Always read books by people who practice what they preach.

You can conquer the world by being noble. Being noble is a virtue. To be an angel you must have passion and grace; don't be a social animal. In the Age of Aquarius there will be no religion. If will be if you experience or not experience. It will be your own spiritual efficiency that is with you. You should know yourself and the truth about yourself. When you have the chance to say something, speak it from your guts and soul. I believe we have had many previous incarnations. Remember a hungry soul can corrupt your mind, body and the way you feel. Don't be afraid to stand out in a crowd of people. You will become more spiritual.

Sometimes you know without direction, without direction you will never find your destiny. People should live their lives with compassion and love. It would be a better world. Some people think they are somebody when they are nobody. If you doubt, you will have pain. We should always be grateful for everything around us. Be kind to yourself and you will be kind to others. Always do everything with grace, this is your identity. Always love yourself.

In life, know who you are, what you want and where you are going. If you want success in life listen to your consciousness. Sometimes you just need to learn to listen. Sometimes people suffer because they don't confront their problems. If you don't want to be forgotten by another person say kind words, they will never forget it. Your body is a temple. Take care of it. When you feel the world is caving in on you, meditate. If we were born to be together then we should enjoy the fruits of life. Always tell the truth, because no matter what, it will come out anyway. We should try to base everything on love. Forgive yourself and your past so you can walk in the light.

Take time throughout the day, for even just a minute, to be you. Feel peace with the universe. To be in a state of tranquility at all times you can flow like water. Whatever you achieve in life is your character. Never think you are perfect. You are. If we forgive our parents many of our burdens will go away.

If you have any trouble just hold your breath for sixteen seconds; your zone and hemispheres will change, your body will know the difference. If you tell people they are beautiful, they don't need makeup. Some people have beauty on the outside but are ugly on the inside. When you start blessing others, you will be blessed. Whatever you can do or experience in life, do it with grace. For the little time we are here, we should leave behind a legacy. Always keep the faith, never give up.

Don't be a slave in your body. Just know you are on a journey going through a planetary shift. Remember we are born to love each other. The act of life is always to serve people. When you start to have greed it creates corruption. Can you understand the "you" within you; feel your own peace and love. Your soul is your life. When there is stress and anger, your life can cause violence. You are in control. Live a life of grace.

Do not cater to your children, they will disobey you and leave home.

The most sensitive part of the body is the eyebrows. Plucking them takes away the electromagnetic field inner current balance. You will never be able to control your health problems.

We have to share our values with the next generation. You can have a relationship with your body and soul. If you are always negative, change your life or you will never change. Meditation can change your state of mind. You should ask yourself who you are- Who am I? Don't ever take advantage of others. Prayer is very powerful. Don't forget to pray. You should judge yourself instead of others that will elevate you. IF you are doing something that doesn't feel right, drop it. With prayer we all live in happiness, love and peace. We should only live for each other, not against them. Wherever you go be the light, be a lighthouse for others. Think more of God.

We are all here to learn and help each other. It is Gods will that we remain free. Your thoughts are very powerful, be careful what you wish for. It isn't what we eat physically; it's what we eat mentally. A woman who plays games is remembered not her identity as a woman. Money does not give you character, it is your characteristics which people trust in you. Believe we all have our own beliefs; it is what you believe in that counts. First know that it is the God within you. That is the power. We are all here for one purpose and that purpose is God.

DON'T DOUBT, TRUST GOD!

CHAPTER 6
"DEATH AND DYING"

Everything in life is a gift from God, and life is the greatest gift of all. Some day we will have to give it back. I feel we are all connected in some way. What you see in others is a reflection of yourself. Don't look at the faults in others; look at your own. It is our destiny and we have control over it. Every action produces a reaction. We reap the consequences of our own actions. All our actions- mental, verbal, and physical- bear fruit. Whatever you sow, you will harvest. If you want to solve a fear, drop it and your problems. Take it to the highest part of you and drop them.

Death is universal and predictable of human existence. We must confront death of our family and friends. The timing of death is the most certain thing in our lives, and is uncertain. We never know when it will come. Death to some people is the indication of human failure. Technology today wizardly regards death as something to be conquered, or delayed at any cost. The old are dying in hospitals and nursing homes, with tubes, dialysis machines. A person on a machine artificially maintained is bizarre.

When my husband was in the hospital the doctor was with him, the phone rang and this doctor told the person, I know he is dead, but keep him on the machine, let the family think he is still alive.

With drugs that dull pain, inhibit awareness of the process of dying. You should confront death entirely unprepared. The mental health profession offered me no psychological help to the dying. In the last decade result of dying research now reviled interest in death and dying among professionals and lay people. You should show respect of people who are dying. In spite of all the work that has been done we have not developed ways to relieve the suffering of those who are dying. In tradition and cultures, knowledge of death is an integral part of the wisdom of life. Ancident death – rebirth mysteries.

Spiritual practices of other great religions share the belief that when we fully accept the morality of the aspect of ourselves, which the ego identifies, we discover that out true identity is eternal and divine. One of the best masters of the oldest most honored spiritual lineage of the east has an entirely different approach, one that is relevant for those leaving us, for those facing imminent death. According to teaching, suffering, weather in life or death, is based on the ignorance of our own real nature and on a false sense of identity. We are filled with fear but once you realize that our identity lies not in the ego or in the body, but in the subtle consciousness that operates both through and beyond physical demise no longer represents to the end of everything. When you get to know your real self not only will the fear of death disappear, but the suffering of life vanishes as well. When you know the Self, both life and death will become enjoyable games.

One Swami describes life and death cycles in terms of doctrine or Karma. The ancient and immutable law of cause and affect which decrees that one must experience the consequences of every action one performs. Birth and dying are part of an endless cycle when we discover the totally free consciousness that exists within us. If we could only liberate ourselves, that energy, called adrenaline, in the ancient Indian texts is recognized in virtually every spiritual tradition as the creative force of energy of the human organism. If a human beings eternal form carries on all the functions of the organism in its internal form, gives rise to the spiritual process. In some people it lays dormant at the base of the spine.

The awakened works on the physical subtle level, burning physical, emotional and mental impurities and ultimately opening the individual to the experience of his or her innate nature can open and free us from the most rooted fears; and open us to undreamed of freedom and joy. When God reveals Himself, within the heart this human being is great; a human being is the highest.

If a person does not know his own inner consciousness, then his life is wasted. It is your duty to find out who you are. Look at your life and everything you have? Are you watching so it does not wither away? When a body is burned it goes up in flames. So why do you think so much of your body, your mind, your wealth? Fear is the last moment and we are afraid to leave it all behind. We fear death for no good reason. You have to have courage and be brave in the face of death. Death is nothing more than a long sleep. In the sleep of death one does not wake up, at least not in the same body.

When a person dies, he or she might see a light or Blue Pearl. This light enters the body when the rhythm of breathing begins. It departs from the body leaving everything limp and lifeless. The blue pearl is at the crown of the head, some people see it when their loved ones die. If a person has committed bad actions, his soul will leave through the anus. According to scripture, it is a sign that this person will go to Hell. If the soul leaved through the eyes this means he has been very virtuous.

Death is one thing in this world that is always on time. When you commit many sins, there is nothing that can be done. When we leave this world we take nothing with us. Our worldly existence here has no value after we leave our bodies. Divine wealth is our love, our compassion for others, our devotion to God. Attain happiness and peace in the world, then when we leave it will go with is. Divine wealth buys God, worldly wealth buys only death.

We reap the consequences of our own actions. This is God's law. We take birth according to our actions. Through meditation, some people see their past lives and for some this is the proof of reincarnation, like you have seen before in meditation. We are born, die, born and die again and again. We transmigrate through different forms, high and low. We exhaust our Karma of the past; we create new Karma for the future. To free yourself, going within and through meditation, discover your own inner self. Then when you are liberated from death, you discard the ego and merge with the Self. The ego is the veil which hides the self helps us bound to the body. The ego is nothing but our sense of limited individuality; our identification with the body and mind.

The purpose of life is to become free of all impurities and perform good actions, not bad action or we will hurt others and ourselves. Once we become full we are nothing but supreme consciousness. In every human being there is a great divine energy called Kundalini that created the whole entire universe in total freedom. I am the self. When you realize that god dwells within you, one's own inner self experiences a new dawn.

The waking and dream states: the witness of our thoughts and feelings is nothing but pure consciousness, the absolute Barhaman (meaning God).

This is what you discover in meditation. When you meditate you move beyond the waking dream and sleep states to that transcending state.

One's condition at the time of death is the result of one's actions. One should understand the value of time. With understanding, meditate and repeat God's name. You can attain everything in this world but once time has passed you cannot get it back. We have made the journey through man lifetimes. We must remember One is God and the other is our own death.

Wake up before death comes to surprise. At the time of death remember God. If you meditate and pray every day you should have no fear of death. Some people forget the reason we come into this world. Desires increase and consume your life. You forget who am I, the goals of your life? What did you accomplish here? To indulge in the sense pleasures, eat and drink and forget the day you will leave this body. The inner self is ageless and unchanging. The supreme truth lies within you; that the light is self. May your awareness turn inward, live with the knowledge, and know you are supreme truth.

When you talk about death I think of my daughter when she died. It was on a Friday evening. I was at a friend's house after dinner and was wrapping the garbage when my thumb started to bleed even though I didn't cut it. I looked at the clock and it bled from 6:20p.m. to 6:50p.m. All I said was God I did nothing wrong but I don't feel good inside. That weekend I knew something happened. On Monday I got a call that my daughter was dead. My daughter was separated from her husband and I couldn't get any information from the police. I called the coroner and told him my daughter died between 6:20 and 6:50 p.m. Friday night. I thought he passed out. No sound. All he said was call the police. I went to the services. When I walked into the funeral parlor her husband was coming out of this room and when he saw me he let out a loud scream. My daughter and I looked alike. I heard that her girlfriends came to her house on Monday and found her dead in the hot tub. They called her husband and said what should we do? She was on strong medication for her rotator cuff. Her mother-in-law told me that my daughter called the police because she wanted her house key. So the police brought the key back at 3:15 p.m. and her husband went over to the house after work because he was mad she called the police for the key. I never got any information from the police because she was still married to him. She never liked hot water, even if we went to a hotel she would sit on a chair while the rest of us went in. She wouldn't even put her feet in.

A few days later I was leaving the house. When I got outside, about 7 am, I t was real bright out. I looked up at the sun and the whole sky was as bright as could be and I felt her presence going toward the light. I felt at peace. A few months later I dreamt if this man picked my daughter up off the couch, she was naked, and he carried her down a hallway. That was the end of the dream.

My husband was older than me and he had health problems later on. He broke his hip and after 9 months was to go in for surgery. I used spiritual healing on his hip every night. When it was time for the surgery the doctor took x-rays. The hip was healed. Other doctors asked me to pray for their loved ones as well.

My husband had surgery, but this time they almost killed him, I had a dream three days before he went to the hospital. I saw this hallway and while he was having surgery it was closed. Seven days later they said they were going to move him into the part of the hospital that I saw in my dream, I knew if they did he would die. I went to the chapel and prayed for three hours, when I went back to see him the nurse said we cannot move him, something came up. I thanked god.

My husband and I were sitting and talking in the hospital. He said his mother came to him and wanted him to go to her. He said no, he was not ready. She came to him again and said she will pray for him. My husband was not a believer of the spirit world, but he was older than me and we were together for thirty years. Three days before my husband's life energy he was in a nursing home and they had to send him to the hospital. I called at 11:00 p.m. and the nurse said that he was doing ok. I said I will come to the hospital because I had always been with him all the years he was in the hospital. The nurse said wait till morning. I got a call at 2:00 a.m. everything was still ok. I went into a deep sleep, the phone rang at 7 a.m. It was the hospital, my husband passed away a few hours before I woke up.

After taking care of him for ten years he was at peace. My sister went to the hospital with me she sat in a chair crying. I was standing next to the bed looking at him; he had an aura white as can be around his head and face. He looked like an angel; I knew his mother was with him to take him home. I told my sister, look, he looks like an angel, but she never looked at me she just sat there. I wanted to touch his face but I couldn't. My friends said, never touch anyone from the spirit world because they have a lot of energy and could give you a heart attack. I kept telling my sister look at him, he looks like an angel. It had to be over one and a half hours that we were there before we left. It just shows how close we are to our loved ones in the spirit world. I saw all this in my dream.

At my husband's funeral, his family was there, but they did not like the age difference between us and his daughter, who is a year older than me, did not care for me at all because she was the one that was going to find the right person for her father when we met. After the service we all go to a restaurant, when I got there my sister said none of Bob's family was coming. I stood like a stone statue. From my waist down I felt like an anchor, from my waist up I felt like I was levitating for a few moments. I told my sister, do I feel great after putting up with his family for thirty years and putting up with his daughter who wanted to control her father.

Before my dad passed away he was in the hospital. He put his hand on my face and I felt this flash of light. Through his hands he gave me a gift before he left this earth plane.

"My Sister"

My sister and I took care of a lady, one week I would go, the next week she would go. I remember it was upstairs in her bedroom. I just stood real still and I said, God, forgive my sister for what she did to me but I knew she was going to die. It was on a Wednesday. I got a call from my other sister saying she had a seizure and was in the hospital. My sister said come to the hospital, I said no, I can pray right here because everyone will be having different thoughts. I never prayed so hard in my life for anyone. My sister had a brain tumor and died one year later. But before she passed away her daughter read her the Mother's Day card she got her. Then my sister opened her eyes of blue and took two breaths and left. I wrote a poem for her.

Sister dear, I love you so, you left this world without a tear.

You gave so much. Now you're gone, your love for life will carry on.

You opened your eyes of blue one more time,
you took two breaths and left.

With grace, love and dignity, God gave you his grace, love and might.

Now you are in the light. I see your face as it shines.

You will come back again, one more time.

I do feel we are all connected in some way and know when something is going to happen. My aunt started and ran Camp Will O Way for twenty-five years for the handicapped, because her daughter was handicapped. I volunteered there at thirteen years old. When her daughter passed away at sixty-one years old a friend of hers who was handicapped was touching the coffin. I told her mother I looked in your daughters eyes and she is an old soul. Her mother said her daughter had one thousand past lives and that they visit the A.R.E. clinic Edgar Cayce foundation. Then she told me her daughter was a healer. Without prayer works are dead.

CHAPTER 7
"THE WISDOM"

It is good every day to have a little wisdom in your life. I feel we are one with everything and all the happiness and honesty are in us, that we can never make a mistake. We must understand our consciousness for what we want to achieve in life. When we live and work with others we need to be more attentive. We need to try to understand the mind of others.

When we have forgiveness in our hearts and compassion, we experience God within. Having faith in any institution you dwell in faith and reason, happiness and radiance will fill that person. We can be healthy, happy, holy so we can smile and shine like the sun to all human beings and have them in the palm of your hand.

Wearing white clothes is good therapy. My friend told me it is the color therapy and we need to be conscious. After a bath it is good to wear white for fifteen minutes. We should discipline ourselves in life, financially, spiritually and physically. If you don't spend enough time on yourself, and your body's needs and feelings, you could be in trouble. Nothing will work.

Try not to challenge phenomena in your life. The outcome could cause pain, disease and misery. I feel every human is God in himself to have compassion and merge with God. I pray that every day peace and joy prevail for all and all experience God's grace. I believe you can make the impossible possible, it sometimes requires commitment and character and protection. Look ahead and see the magnetism in you. If you have a problem, chisel it away and you will get an answer.

Change your food, chew your food well and mix it with saliva. You will become healthier! Your brain will be sharper. Love is a force to experience your higher consciousness for loving yourself, your inner being, to master the highest stage of love within you. When you meditate you gain a lot, more achievements can manifold. Think well of yourself and others.

It is sometimes hard to avoid pressure in your everyday life- makes being single, married or death a difficult job- choose right from wrong. It is the way you want to go and for your children the most serious part is your direction choosing right from wrong. Doing a lot of selfless service is a test of selflessness and putting your life on the path of righteousness. When you seek to someone with grace, that grace will come back to you.

In life you should be wise, essential: how you protect the self. If you do not protect the self, you will always live in self-conflict. Having faith is a very powerful institution. When you dwell in logic, faith and reason the argument leaves and happiness and radiance will fill the person.

In all that you do show the spirit of God, of being right, and flow of nature. If you can do that it is meditation.

Always ask for strength and courage so you can elevate yourself to be healthy, happy, holy, and blessed with our lives and be as this spirit shining for all human beings.

Sing songs. It is a beautiful emotional release. You will be so grateful to yourself. It's a way to stay sane, another way to confront insanity.

Music is good for the soul. Be careful what you do in life because it takes forty days to get a reputation, then twenty-five years to get rid of it.

If you commit yourself and life, that life, as a commitment, you will find absolute infinite freedom.

Pray that God will bless us with his grace and give us knowledge and wisdom; to have light and remove darkness; to have compassion, to control our passion; to serve everyone with grace and love; to speak the truth at all times so we can live in peace.

Love is so powerful. When you have that love you can move mountains. Love can never be forgotten. No one can change your character when you are an honest person. Never make any changes. Just know that God is beautiful, bountiful and wonderful and he created you. When you commit yourself to serve in any way, do it with love, kindness and affection. It will satisfy you and give you trust.

Life is a gift. It is essential energy. Life is a gift from God face to face.

I feel in my heart God and I are basically the same like two sides of a coin. Forget the past or you will never have a future. Do not look back. You have to develop your own meditative mind.

God gave us the power to desire. Whatever you desire you need to be able to control. Always give yourself a chance. Count you diversions and always direct your energy in God's way. You will find peace, happiness, prosperity and joy.

To understand your existence you are honest, to speak the truth because we were born with the truth.

When you sit in a room with other people and you talk about God, love and elevation, you manifest God. We can all do wrong. We can try to do it right. In my heart I don't feel we should kill or punish a person; find wrong and make it right. This is called the flow if life. I pray one day we will all be awakened to a higher consciousness.

Always know you are the will of god. Getting up in the morning is a act, but it is a personal strength for sharpness and discipline. You always heard life is a play. Your mission if life is to understand that whatever you do keep guiding all coming generations. Trust in God you dwell in God.

Self-discipline is not a project. You must have discipline or you may grow up the wrong way. Love yourself so you have freedom, liberation, and ecstasy. Accept your life is very sacred. Prayer is powerful and so is love. We are all part of the universe and the magnetic field. The way we feel is our choice that matters and God's plan.

Religion is a family of God; religion is a state of consciousness.

If this religion does the job; how can you be depressed all together? Forgiveness is the highest performance and the direct approach to life. If someone is wrong don't let it remain wrong. To achieve a desire you have to have commitment and the will to fulfill it. May god guide you, protect you, that you grow in grace. May you shine like the sun and know all.

When you are spiritual you do not react or be afraid.

Remember you are what you relate to, don't limit yourself or you will be limited. Universal, obey, serve and love. Religions will change; prophets will come and go, merge in God and obey this law. Pray for peace, strength and grace. Leave your problems by serving and uplifting others. If you are positive you have the power to think who you really are and what you can do. When that special moment comes, listen and be the truth.

Everyone has been blessed in body, mind and soul. This is the highest when your body and mind can serve the soul. Everyone has a beautiful soul. All you have to do is get in touch with it. Sometimes we are tested in life to allow you standards to be tested. See God in all and serve God in all.

Life is a gift that lives on. Any challenge in life has to be met. It is a test of the human dignity. This life is not about you. It is about your spirit. If you have fear or are afraid, say "NO". God will take care of you. Trust God.

Wisdom comes from knowledge, just know it. Things may change in your life whatever it may be. What you wear, eating habits, social behavior and your destiny.

In the Age of Aquarius everyone will be the leader of his or her own spirit. You will be in control of your own life. I pray each day that God will raise us up higher and higher, to give us the strength and courage to be humble, to serve and reach out to all. There is good and bad in the world but choose the right way with a smile and grace, that people know that they can trust you.

Just a marriage is an elevated state to be in where two people become One Divine Being. When you take time to meditate you can empty yourself and let the universe come to you.

To serve mankind we should use our present hospitality and service to serve all mankind with grace and love

When you think with your head, think with your heart. When you think with your heart, think with your head. I pray to God to bless us and rise above everything that we can, serve, be truthful, humble, strong, and smile to make this a better world.

If you worry you have to concentrate, it is physical. Use your mind to the universal mind, things will come to you. "This is true".

Whenever you receive a gift, thank God it becomes fate. If you do not give thanks it becomes a curse. Note that we all were born with "X", the gift amount of breath. But if you breathe faster, you will lose your life earlier. If you see someone falling apart try to put them together. Just don't let him fall, and that way you can keep yourself from falling.

Always try to meditate on God to transform him from "I" to "We" in life here, and the hereafter. You can lose weight by working on your metabolism and your glandular system; get started with a Guru or a yoga teacher. You should have self-knowledge like lighting a candle. Once you light it, all darkness goes away. Just love yourself, and then you can love everyone.

God is within you. Our God will not abandon you. If God is for you who can be against you? When we are still and silent you can receive all knowledge. To have knowledge is to develop faith in you. You should have enough grace in your heart to fill the entire universe. Like the smell of a rose, it is do powerful, but your grace should be so powerful that people want to feel it. Jesus Christ said you should have enough faith as a mustard seed. Be firm in your faith. Do everything with love.

When two are in a relationship there should not be any agony. You should honor your word. Don't lower each other. Be kind and gentle. You took a vow to respect it. Hugging is so good for the soul. If you cannot hug yourself, you cannot hug another.

CHAPTER 8
MY EXPERIENCES

Only read books that people have experience with.

My first experience was at seven years old when I made my first communion. I did not believe in confession. When I was nine years old my grandma was cleaning her dresser drawer, as I was sitting on the bed watching her I saw a Rosary and a prayer book. I said, "Grandma when you die, will you send me three roses so I know you are in heaven"? Thirteen years later my husband and I went to breakfast at my parents. I rang the bell and my mom came to the door with the Sunday paper. My mom said, "Look at this. A man got up in the morning and when he was coming down his living room steps, he saw three roses on his living room floor, but did not know how they got there". But through this man, the media, my mom, I know my grandma was in heaven. It took three people to get in touch with me through the spirit world.

A friend of mine, of over thirty years, was eighty-two and still working at a school. She asked me to make two keys for her and bring them over on Monday because her children were coming from out of town and she was going to the hospital on Tuesday. I told my mom if something good doesn't happen to her, she will commit suicide. On Monday I tried three times to go over to her house, something always came up. I did get the keys made and went over to her house about 3:00 PM. We had dinner together and I said I'd see her in the hospital. She said wait, I got a social security card in

the mail today with my husband's name on it. I said to her, you are really
losing it, why would you get a social security card at eighty-two years old?
I called social security right away and the man I talked to told me it was a
mystery, no one sent her a card.

I took the card from her and put it on the table and all of a sudden
got all this energy in my body that I could have taken her house right off
the foundation. I said your husband is with us, he is right here next to my
right side. I kept repeating to her can't you feel his presence? She looked
at me like I'd lost it. I took her hand and she was levitating. She stood in
front of me and I took my hand away and she sat down and said why did
he wait so long and pills were not the way out. She started laughing, I said
call your sister and tell her, and they both started laughing and said I'll go
to the hospital I don't care what happens. She was in the hospital for four
days and I could not get a chance to visit her, something always came up.
When she god home I said I was sorry for not visiting her in the hospital.
She said that was okay, my loved ones from the spirit world were with me.
She was never a believer. That night I went to bed and I was still filled with
a lot of energy and fell asleep.

One summer I was at my parents' house for a cookout, it was the
evening when everyone left. I took a bath, when I got out of the tub to dry
off I felt hands on my shoulders, but I was alone in the room. The hands
moved me out of the bathroom, down the hallway and into my bedroom
in front of my dresser where I had my jewelry box. When I opened it I
saw that my wedding rings were missing. I started to cry and went into
the living room where both my parents were sitting. I said someone took
my wedding rings. I called my friend and she did a reading for me- the
drawing was a house with a lot of steps and the ring would be in a vase on
top of a refrigerator. I had my dad take me to this person's house and he
tried to get her out of the kitchen but it did not work. Months later I heard
that her husband had wedding rings for sale.

My friend said another teacher was coming through in tulip time. I
was told good things will come to you and I will be on the inside looking
out.

Some friends moved away, and it was a half-year later and I felt her
husband needed prayers. So every morning when I had breakfast and
prayed for the world, I would pray for him. Two weeks later I got a letter.
Her husband needed surgery, they took a test before the surgery and told
her that he didn't need the surgery anymore. She said I know it was your
prayers.

This ladies son told his dad that he wanted to be a basketball coach. His dad said no, no future in it. One day I did some spiritual healing on him and told him go with you heart, he did and became a basketball coach at a college for years, if he still is I do not know.

One day this lady I knew said she did not believe in god. She needed help with her daughter so she went to this one church, but they turned her away and she committed suicide. The time I was with her she started believing again.

About two years after I was married I was lying in bed alone. My son was two months old and my German Shepard dog was on the floor next to him. It was spring, it was twilight time outside and the whole room was a dead still. I looked to my right side and was a person standing next to me, just a form of a person. At first I thought it was my father-in-law or someone playing a joke on me. It just stood there and left. Six months later I got a divorce. One year later I saw it again, but it kept coming back to when something was going on in my life.

Later on I married an older man and told him about it but he could never see it. This person was there when I had surgery a few times. I always heard a dark person was on the negative side so I went to a preacher and he said it was Satan taking the form of a person. He was coming more and more. Maybe he was saying he wasn't Satan. After six years I willed it away. But no harm ever came to me. I'm sure when the time comes he will show himself and who he is.

One evening I was taking a bath and I was in a twilight sleep. I started to slide under the water when I felt someone from the spirit world grab my left arm and pull me up before I went under. I thanked them for being there.

I volunteered at this one hospital for twenty-five years. One night I was working in the gift shop, a lady about thirty five came in and she was crying. I asked her if I could help her. She said her dad was in the hospital, but it was her husband and he was from another country and her son was in college and he was very hard on him. All of a sudden I said to her if your husband does not change his ways, your son will commit suicide.

I worked at a group home when I was fifteen. People would hear children running around at night. Some aides would see a woman in a gown walking the halls at night. Many strange things went on there. It used to be an old farm house and had a barn outside next to a park.

After my sister passed away her daughter has a little girl years later. She was now two years old, we were all at an outing. Everyone went into the house and I was with her daughter. She was in a walker. All of a sudden she looked at me and just as fast as she could move she started coming at me with her hands moving all over the place. She scared the heck out of me. I just moved back because she kept coming toward me. The whole family believes my sister came back. She was trying to tell us she came back. She sure got my attention.

A friend of mine was having a barbeque grill built, the man who was building it said he needed five hundred dollars more for material. He took the money and never came back. My friend called the police and the officer said that everyone was looking for him, even the state patrol. I started to pray every morning while I had my breakfast that God never made a dishonest or greedy man. That divine love met and always will meet any human need. I prayed for over a year. One weekend I was out at his house, it was on a Thursday night. I told him, "You will get you money back this weekend". At 6:30 pm Saturday night a car pulled up to his house, it was the police officer. He handed my friend an envelope containing five hundred dollars, the police officer told us that the man had turned himself in.

On the weekends I would cook at a group home. On occasion I would take my friends dog to visit with the residents there and he would go to all the residents but one. I knew this lady had some psychic abilities. When I started to leave and say my good-byes there she was standing by the door. I was shocked to see her standing. This woman had to have someone help her all the time, she never walked alone. All of a sudden I looked into her eyes. I heard a woman's voice saying, get me out of here. This woman kept repeating it. This ladies hair was gray and short, but I saw her with brown hair styled like a pageboy. I stepped back and said God, what can I do? She is in a group home how am I supposed to get her out of here? This woman was over eighty years old. She never talked. Again I heard the voice, "Get me out of here". I was ready to leave and so was the dog that was as far away from her as he could get.

I asked God, what can I do for her and the other people? This woman who owned the group home was starving the residents and much more was going on. I reported her to a lawyer of our city, at the time he said he would put it in a personal file and it will stay there. I called another place and was told to leave, I said no. The owner was closed down and the people where moved to better places.

A friend of mine has a bakery in an old building on the south side of Milwaukee. The family that she bought it from went up north for vacation.

While driving home a train was coming and the father wanted to beat it, but the train beat him and his whole family dies. Now you see the little girl in the basement of the bakery, and I saw the presence of a large man. One of the girls started work at 5:30 am and she heard a noise and saw the little girl in a dress. The little girl asked, "Am I dead"? She did not know what to say. I told her the next time you see her tell her yes and to go home. The other help sees her too. I would say she is around 10 years old with long hair to her shoulders.

I took my mom to a club I belonged to that was having a dance. I was watching people dancing and this couple was coming off the dance floor and I told my mom that the man was going to die soon. Two weeks later I heard the man was outside with his wife doing yard work. He told her he was going inside to lie down. When his wife came in he had already passed away. This was exactly two weeks after the dance.

When my mom broke her hip she had to go to the nursing home for rehab. The second night there she was having dinner and said she needed her sweater. I told her I would get it, on the way back this lady who was taking care of another woman asked why my mom was there. I said we were at a theater, she went to the bathroom and I felt that she was going to fall on her way back. I saw her coming toward us and I got up and the feeling went away. When she got to the row we were sitting in she fell and fractured her hip. The woman asked, "What do you see in me". I didn't say anything and she asked a second and third time while standing in front of me. I just looked at her and saw a black aura around her. I started to tell her many things about a man she knew. What I told her was not good. She said she was kicking her boyfriend out. I heard months later she went back to her old ways.

One time I was with my mom and these children were playing a golf game called 'A Hole in One'. No one could do it. About a half hour later I told my mom that the girl is going to do it. She did and got a bottle of soda for free.

My friend who adopted me in her heart brought me up with Edgar Cayce. (It made my life much better and different ways of thinking and for the healing I got from her and those in the spirit world and from Edgar Cayce.) My friend said she was coming back to me through a trumpet. She also said someday everyone will be a golden tan. I was told take your money out of the bank, it will not be any good. Her son to is very special to me and he is special in his own way.

I was cleaning the oven one day; I picked up the burner that was still hot. All I could think of was my friend. I called her on the phone and she said to think of her brother. He was killed in a fire and to call back in fifteen minutes. When I called her back the redness and pain on my hand was gone, she said an Indian was standing at her side from the spirit world. My friend was Indian and French. She has spiritual insights as I would say E.S.P. Extra Sensory Perception, awareness of or response to our external or influence not apprehended by sensory means.

A.   Telepathy, thought, transference.
B.   Clairvoyance; the power of discerning.
C.   Precognition; seeing the future.
D.   Post-Recognition; seeing into the future.
E.   Psychogenesis; the effects of the mind on an object.

This is what my friend told me about E.S.P.

My friend gave me this prayer to say. It is a beautiful Sioux Indian Prayer.

Oh Great Spirit whose voice I hear in the windows, whose breath gives life, to all the world hear me.

I come before you, one of your many children.

I am small and weak I need your strength and wisdom.

Let me walk in beauty and make my eyes ever behold the red purple sunset.

Make my hands respect the things you have made.

Make my ears sharp to hear your voice.

Make me wise so that I know the things you have taught my people.

The lessons you have hidden in every leaf and rock.

I seek strength not to be superior to my people, but to be able to fight my greatest enemy, myself.

Make me ever ready to come to you with clean hands and straight eyes, so when life fades as a fading sun sets my spirit may come to you without shame.

Amen.

A friend of mine invited me to his home. He said to come on Friday and leave on Saturday. I said," No I want to come on Thursday and leave on Friday." I finally agreed to come on Friday and leave on Saturday. I had a dream 3 days before I was going to his house. I was going under a bridge, my car got out of control, spun around a few times and went back under the bridge and scraped the whole front end. I got out of the car. I saw the car it was white and I was not hurt.

I went to my friend's house Friday and left on Saturday. On the expressway home the dream came true. The car got out of control. I hit something, black ice, I don't know for sure because I couldn't see anything on the road. My car spun around, hit the side of the bridge and scraped the whole front end. I got out. I was ok: I saw it was a white car like in my dream that I just bought three days before. I could not figure out why this busy expressway was like a dead still around me. For about fifteen minutes there were no cars, as if God had stopped all the traffic.

CHAPTER 9
YOGA

Yoga is the oldest science known to man. Yoga is for women, men and children of any age. When you define Yoga, it is unity or joining together.

Using age is an excuse; age is only a state of mind. Yoga is derived from the Sanskrit root meaning bind yoke. It is a union of our will and the will of God, yoking all the powers of the body, mind and soul to God. It means disciplining of the intellect. It means a poise of the soul which enables one to look at life in all its aspects harmoniously. Yoga is not a religion in itself. It is a way of life so you can attain a deeper, fuller understanding of your own religious beliefs.

Yoga brings health and wellbeing to each individual. Yoga tones the body and will give you more energy, vitality and an overall improvement. Yoga is the understanding of the human form and how to preserve the health and youthfulness of one's self. It is through Yoga that you will gain the knowledge to create the happy, healthy body and mind.

Meditation is a powerful tool for quieting the mind and effortlessly turns back towards itself. (Edgar Cayce, who was a great prophet and psychic call this the "Magic Silence".) Twenty minutes in the morning and twenty minutes in the evening.

Breathing: Breath unlocks the power of energy when the body opens the channels to replenish the flow of external energy. To learn to breathe is to lean to live. Breath gets rid of tension and many other problems. There are over 100 ways to breathe. Breath cures all.

Through Yoga many things happen. When you have spiritual powers you shine like the sun and know all, but you must use these powers in the right way. Everything is a state of mind. When you wake up you'll see this world is only an illusion, only a dream. When your mind is truthful all your actions will bear positive fruit immediately. When man lives and entertains the truth alone, he becomes a source of enlightenment to all others.

Everything we experience is the self. Tell yourself you are aware of the self and who you are. Yoga can bring internal harmony control over the nervous system and conservation of energy. Yoga will develop poise, balance, flexibility and ability to relax. It will give you a better outlook on life, better health. Your attitude has everything to do with your life, when negative thoughts come into your mind change it to a positive one right away or your problem will just get bigger. Just a little bitterness and anger will stop the flow of energy and destroy the cells. Anxiety stress is based on belief of limitations. We do Yoga, that is a storehouse of impressions, can be burnt up. As we need grace from a great being. We all need the grace of God. We all need self-discipline, meditating ego and renunciation. By purifying the mind one starts to know the nature of God. Go beyond your fears, conflicts and desires so you can experience the self within.

Yoga strengthens the body and mind and your body has a pattern of its own and established aging process. Yoga makes people live longer. Yoga stimulates abdominal muscles, spine, lungs, pelvic area, refreshes the glands and nerve centers with pranic energy from the disciplined breathing. Yoga therapy automatically brings you into a state of mind to perfectly attend your own psychoanalyst. Yoga is a union of body and mind.

When breathe is irregular the mind is unsteady. When breathe is still so is the mind. Still Yoga obtains the power of stillness. The Asanas postures will refine your inner and outer spaces, as well as harmonize the life giving systems of the body. When you think you can't do any more with the body, you can still get breath benefits in just a few postures. This Asanas posture is to restore energy.

Become liberated while living. Perform your duty. Don't worry about the future. You can practice Yoga; every move takes you through a limitation to a new sense of freedom. The practice of Yoga is to merge this illusionary self, the ego or self. That is the way man is subject to external births and deaths, because man's idea is to attempt to satisfy and fulfill itself. The meaning of Yoga is to merge the illusionary self with the ocean of universal mind. So cause and effect cease to be a reality and true peace is experienced. To achieve this liberation we engage in the practice of both physical and mental discipline.

There is no such thing as failure in Yoga, just degrees of success. This success depends on the time and effort you devote to your practice. (With Yoga and meditation you are making a very wise decision.) Many things can happen through Yoga.

The life force in you when you when in the company of certain people, those who do not have their own organisms, draw on the vitality of those around them; be with people who have much more life force. We talk a lot but say very little. Some people depend on the T.V, or radio to keep their senses occupied. The entertainment makes you restless, tense and emotionally strained and drained. So many things in life today take your energy. You should try to avoid it whenever possible. Don't worry what other people think of you. Just pay attention to your own emotional body.

Yoga Philosophy and Meditation

Yoga is man's oldest known method of scientifically dealing with the self. You waste your life force by nervous habits, being with negative people, idle talk, misuse of your senses, smoking, pacing, chewing gum, expression of fear, anger , anxiety and other unhealthy mental emotional conditions.

You have to learn to relax with your activities. Haven't you always heard, make every move count? Take lessons from the cat. He moves, stretches, relaxes and naps. The cat does not waste energy. You can learn from him about conservation.

Everyone wants to be happy and get the most out of life. We want contentment and peace of mind and soul while discontentment is all around us. Money and fame do not bring us closer to the peace within us that we seek. (Sometimes we go through life in what seems to promise relief.) Sooner or later none of these things can help us with the ultimate peace that we seek, all these things are substitutes. It attempts to treat the symptoms, not the real cause. If we have peace of mind, body and spirit we could pierce through the heart of the matter.

Through Yoga we can learn different levels of consciousness and sub consciousness that refer to as universal mind. All problems, confusion, suffering in life stems from the fact that we do not understand the nature of our ordinary mind, that we possess the power of the universal mind.

Ordinary mind had taken over our lives. It is our higher consciousness that we find ourselves in the most perplexing circumstances beset by problems which seem to have no solution.

Some of us are not aware of the existence of the universal mind and do not know how to use it. Use your mind to lead you down the path of faith, peace and fulfillment. Don't chase after empty promises. Keep hoping for success. If you have not fulfilled yourself it can lead you to blame it on every conceivable outside circumstance, then you say it's bad luck. You fail because it is misunderstood workings of our ordinary mind. Everyone is looking for the pot of gold at the end of the rainbow. What we see is part of a circle. In Yoga we use the symbol of a wheel that we call the wheel of life.

Each of us has to pass through all the possible conditions of the human existence, night and day and drink the waters that truly satisfy thirst.

ALL TRUTH AND WISDOM
ARE UNIVERSAL MIND

Some people don't think that the ordinary mind creates our problems and then, in its own good time, solves them on the outside. So is a game that will continue to play as you allow it to do so. With meditation you will come to understand that you are not the ordinary mind and that has not nearly the importance which we attach to it.

Knowing how to concentrate will open up new facilities of mind; give insight on how to accomplish what you want most with minimum effort. When you have extra hours don't clutter your mind with idle daydreams, wishful thinking or the past and future. It is an illusionary flash way to see the world and ourselves in relation to it. It takes a lot of life force to think the mind is like a record that plays over and over again.

Meditate during your daily activities; try to withdraw yourself from this world of activity for a period of time each day. You have to become the master of your mind and not the slave. It has to take orders, not giving them. You have to understand yourself to find peace of mind and spirit to lead to a richer life.

We have to stop the body from being tense, unnecessarily strained, as it is draining our vital energies. We have to learn that the ordinary mind is needlessly sapping our life force by allowing it to run wild without control. Observe your mind. Notice if it has been concentrated on what you're doing.

Yoga has changed people's lives from the ancient science, which restores health, vigor and youth. Yoga is a physical and spiritual experience. Yoga can build and restore vitality and body harmony. I am glad one of my teachers was the first to bring Yoga to the states. India is the land of origin. Many men and women in movies of the western world stood on their heads and did Yoga. If you are Jewish, Christian or whatever, Yoga does not have an effect on one's own faith. Just as holding the breath can recharge the body. You feel a little light headed but it can open your psychic development. Yogis become clairvoyant concentrating on recharging the body.

When I meditate on my true self and my dreams many things come true through my dreams. Using the word Om, the supreme word of God, can signify all of nature as the universe; a sacred word you can meditate on. "Just as man must raise himself by his own efforts, be his own friend, or he alone is his worst enemy." Many of the exercises combined with the breathing build up resistance and relieve certain psychosomatic symptoms, past lives for some misfortunes or evil, the better ones left, the higher development next time around.

Watch your thoughts are not far away. Be careful what you wish for, even your parents. Some people do not believe after death we return again. I believe my sister who passed on came back and her daughter is now her mother.

Healing people from miles away just by meditation and prayer can heal them. Some friends of mine moved miles away and it was a little over a year when one morning I felt he needed prayer. I prayed every morning for a week. Two weeks later I received a letter in the mail from his wife saying that the morning he was to have surgery they took a test and he did not need the surgery anymore. I knew it was your prayers. Prayer is powerful.

We should think more of the beauty around us in every form, nature, and of people and their problems. We should think more of the universe and its many wonders; the animals, flowers, and trees. All creatures have life, all in the natural rhythm of life. Always stay in tune with the universe and God.

The efforts you make to find yourself, with your own faith, will be its own reward. Yoga can do a lot for you. You will be less critical, have more compassion, be more understanding, smile and be more open to others. Reincarnation- people know that life doesn't begin at birth or end at death. It is the acts we have previous existences.

Meditating on God, I know that all things are possible for God, and then possible for me to finish this life before the new kingdom comes 2021. Man was a mysterious marvel, between time and space. We have to awake and get out of the slumber, the power limitlessness of everyone's struggles for health to conquer the body and soul, like a flower unfolding, letting the sunshine come in. Some people keep blinders on all material things. Those who are more spiritual for a more beautiful and higher life, say the greatest mind on Earth is man. Man has tried to solve the mystery and the greatest secret there is; oneself.

Just as Hatha Yoga, HA-SUN, THA-MOON, Joining, Yoke, it is the perfect knowledge of the two energies, positive sun and the negative moon energies joining in perfect harmony.

Hatha Yoga helps us to utilize and store the free flow of the life force to the maximum extent. Since man is spirit clothed in flesh and within himself reflects the laws of spirit and body. Positive energy is life giving. Heavy eating and drinking, the physical side causes of obesity and mental obtuseness that upset the individual's equilibrium.

Some people do not believe a higher self that opens the way for the eternal source of strength that dwells within their soul. Some people lack self-confidence and then he becomes powerless and helpless. Some people lack self-confidence and then he becomes powerless and helpless. You will succeed if you believe in what you are doing and have enough self-confidence to master all difficulties.

The greatest teacher in the world is Jesus Christ. Remember what he said, who came out of the east. "Take no thought for your life, what ye shall eat or what ye shall drink; nor yet for your body, ye shall put on. So not the life more than meat and body more than raiment? Behold the fowls of the air; for they sow not, neither do they reap, no gather into bins; Yet your heavenly father feedeth them. Are ye not much better than they?

I saw Jesus Christ in a dream. Our minds collect data from reincarnations; we are here now to better ourselves, our personality and higher self. Hatha Yoga shows us how to keep order from the forces that animate the body, and that we have sinned against our health. Through Yoga, you can start a better healthy you. Open yourself to a higher awareness psychic enfoldment to control your life and your world as never before. Get rid of fear, sins and mental blocks. Everything we have now is here for a reason. Free yourself now.

A yoga pose Matsydsana, Matsya mean fish. Matsya the fish is an incarnation of Visnu, the source and maintainer of the universe and of all things is related. Once upon a time the whole earth had become corrupt and was about to be overwhelmed by a universal flood. Visnu took form of a fish and warned Manu, the Hindu Adam, of the impending disaster. The fish carried Manu, his family and the seven great sages in a ship fastened to a horn on his head. It also saved the Veda from the flood. We are all connected in some way.

Meditation releases you of all tension and distress. Take deep breaths through the nose, take deep breaths expanding your consciousness. Close your eyes. Concentrate, relax the mind. Open your heart to Christ's presence and his angels of light. Relax. Let go. Now rest in God's love and peace nourishing your spirit within this blessing, it cleanses and steadies the mind, uplifting and healing your spirit within. "Now you are everywhere, everything". You should get a good Guru or teacher to help you with Yoga and breathing.

One who practices Kundalini Yoga, 108 elements in the universe including a conscious creation of the creator. Kundalini Yoga is not a religion; religions were created from it. Kudalini Yoga is not a fad, not a cult. It is a practice of experience of a person's own doormat excellence that is awakened. We are now entering the Age of Aquarius. It will be a new time. The entire psyche is changing. You must purify your mind, body and soul to be real. You have to elevate yourself to be angelic. This age will serve is in an age of awareness and experience.

Humming the word OM you will experience a different sound and vibration and begin to say it faster. Just the word Om with humming sound calms the mind, opens the brain waves to reach out into the universe. Everything comes from the word Om or springs from the word OM.

Healing the wounds of love brings us to life, gives us courage to live our lives. It inspires us to sacrifice our lives for others. As natural as love is, so are the wounds of life. Live carefully. You need to learn how to heal the wounds of love. You have to heal old wounds which were broken.

Start your morning with a cup of joy. Tell yourself I'm happy, I'm healthy, I'm holy. Start seeing good in yourself and the universe. Unfold peace and harmony. Be careful who your friends are. They reflect you and you reflect them. Bow to yourself and thank yourself. Keep your mind under control at all times, no matter how things go. You must remain calm, quiet and peaceful. This peace is the source of prosperity. It is the highest spiritual strength. There is nothing to match it. Don't run away from your problems. Face them. Say this is my fear, I am afraid of this fear. It will melt away into nothingness.

The past is dead. This is the present and the future will take care of itself. Keep your mind under control. By letting go it all gets done. This world was won by those who let go.

Some people have a chip on their shoulder. People should behave rightly toward the rest of the world. Fill your cup. (Yesterday that seemed not important exists not.) Fill your cup with love of life and success. Forget the failures and trials that were burned yesterday. The future will take care of itself.

My sister gave me a cup of soup and I returned the cup empty. So she called me and said you did not fill the cup. I said God can fill it with a lot more than I can. Three hours later she called me and said we just sold our house. I said see, I told you God can fill it more than I can. Just be relaxed and free and God will work wonders for thee.

You can chant a Yoga sound in a humble state of mind. After all that is said and done, never expect anyone to respect you with such a state of mind. One can chant the Yoga sound.

The end and the new dawn 2021

The only miracle is unity:

With the creator and all creation.

"Whatever you do, do it consciously. Do not lose your awareness. The day will certainly come when you awake to the self. And then the entire world will be illumined. Actually, it is already illumined, and when you attain that light you will experience it as your own."

AWAKE! REJOICE! LIFE IS A GIFT!

CHAPTER 10

DREAMS

Almost all of my dreams are in color. Edgar Cayce came to me many times. One time he told me to pray for this country. In another dream he came back and told me to pray for the tribes. When people come to you from the spirit world they tell you different ways how they come across. Like my friend, she would do drawings of hearts and circles for months, everyone is different. The readings that she did were very beautiful. One night she was a reading and I told her not tonight. She said sit down; all that came through was, Good night. As for me, it just happens. I don't know when or why, I just tell them whoever is coming through me in the spirit world. Sometimes when I am walking I will start to levitate a few inches of the ground.

I had a dream that lasted three nights in a row; it was always the same two men. I saw Jesus Christ in a dream. I was sitting in a chair facing north. He was very beautiful, his clothes were blue and white and flowing.

A Guru came to me in a dream, carried me over a stream to his room and said it was a small room because we are only here for a short time. He took me back to the stream and on my right side I saw these people with white clothes on. It was very peaceful and beautiful. I hope this is going to be like 2021.

In another dream there were three Indians. Two were on horseback with their beautiful headdresses and clothes. As they were riding off they stopped and looks back, then kept going. The third Indian was very old sitting on the ground with his beautiful clothes and headdress. He was a chief. He said he was tired so I sat down with him.

My sister called me and told me Beaver died. He killed himself. A few weeks later he came to me in a dream and said someone had a gun to his head (a figure of speech). He looked so pure and had a beautiful light around him. Three months later he came back to me in another dream and said everything was ok.

Months after my husband died he came to me in a dream. We were in a car by a bridge and got out. He was hanging over the bridge with his hands just holding on. I just stood for a while and at first did not want to do it. But I took his fingers off the bridge so he could let go, and leave this world. Ten years after his death he finally let go.

In one dream I saw this girl, very beautiful with blond hair. I asked what her name was because my friend said my angel would be a girl. She said her name was Allison.

In one dream a voice told me the cure for epilepsy is "theoshane", theo means God, Shane means nature.

One dream I was swimming in a pool. I was holding this young boy about eight years old. As I was holding in my arms his face was in the water and he was wearing a black suit. Just then the phone rang and I said," Hello, Hello", there was a lot of static on the phone, I kept saying hello. Then a man's voice said it was in the lining. He said goodnight. I have never ever heard a voice like that. It was different and pure. I called the ARE clinic and talked to someone I knew and told him what happened. He told me Edgar Cayce always wondered about talking to those in the spirit world. I'll never forget his voice. As my friend always told me, we would talk to our loved ones through a phone.

Another dream I was in a hallway with a few people and a fire started. Everyone get out, I was at the end and the fire got bigger. I started to walk through the hall I saw that it wasn't a fire at all. It was just silver foil or aluminum foil, just a state of mind.

I fly a lot in my dreams, even if it's from one block to the next.

I dreamt of Michel Landon from' Little House on the Prairie'. He was sitting by a window just looking out. He looked at peace.

I dreamt of Elvis Presley a few months after he died. He was walking on a beach he was at peace, it was a beautiful day.

I kept a journal and recorded a lot of my dreams.

November 1987- I dreamt of peace in the world.

November 11987- One of Edgar Cayces family came to me in a dream.

January 7, 1981- I was at a birthday party and my grandma was with us, but she already passed away.

January 26, 1981- The dream was Atlanta, Georgia killings and I saw the person who did it.

January 12, 1981- Natalie wood. I saw just her head lying there.

January 14, 1981- Paul Lynn was sitting with me when I was at the Performing Arts Center

January 17, 1981- Frank from Hill Street Blues.

January 19, 1981- Bob Hope was in a dream a few times. James Cagney was to me.

January 24, 1981- I found a silver cross with a Madonna on it.

January 26, 1981- Sylvester Stallone we were very happy and he was very nice to me.

January 28, 1981- Linda Evens, I know she was going to break up with this one man. Two weeks later she did.

February 2, 1981- I saw two books by July 6, gold old fashioned cover three inches high and an old fashioned lady on the cover. They were books for the future to communicate with the spirit world through telephones.

February 3, 1981- Bing Crosby

February 6, 1981- Shirley on T.V from 'Laverne and Shirley'.

February 7, 1981- Phil Donahue show.

February 9, 1981- An angel of mercy came to me three times.

February 10, 1981- I saw a lot of war equipment, reds.

February 11, 1981- Prince Charles, Diana was pregnant. It was a false pregnancy.

February 13, 1981- A basketball team was going on strike.

February 14, 1981- I was in an old house from 1800 to 1900. One room is where a man died.

February 17, 1981- The girl on the Charmin tissue. I saw her parents.

February 21, 1981- I was in the service. I told the person in charge about a nuclear war.

July 2, 1982- I was in church with a microchip. Some men were after me for it. I could blow up the world. I handed it to the priest. It was silver with dots or holes 2X2 wrapped around it.

July 4, 1982- I dreamt of my dad. He has a green shirt on and kissed me. Then he passed out all these gifts at Christmas.

July 10, 1982- I saw three flying saucers all around the sky and one split into two. One a bright light and round, the light when under water and the water and the water got real high. My friend told me I would see three flying saucers. That was in 1963.

July 18, 1982- I had two pots of chili on the stove. They floated to the ground.

July 21, 1982- The Bermuda Triangle is a dangerous place. A turtle told me this. I kept him warm and fed him.

July 25, 1982- I was flying all around in my dream.

July 30, 1982- Edgar Cayce came to me again and told me to bless this country. I woke up at 6:30 a.m. right after he told me this. I felt his presence on my left side. (You will never know who in the spirit world will come to you and why.)

August 2, 1983- My sister-in-law was in a nursing home where I volunteered at. I went to visit her and she was in a wheel chair. Two days later I dreamt of her and she was in her wheelchair, she stood up and floated away. They next day I called a friend of mine who ran the home. I asked if my sister-in-law passed away at 1:00 a.m. She said yes. It was beautiful and spiritual.

August 4, 1983- I dreamt I left this earth plane and came back to live with peace and love and harmony and beautiful fields with others.

August 6, 1983- Abraham Lincoln looked like he was 5'3" and thin. I touched his feet and he was funny.

August 10, 1983- I saw Cleopatra in Rome. There was a little boy in bed and he said he was sick and dying. He had another brother. He was the better one. I saw pink ashes and I touched them.

August 12, 1983- I saw a UFO in the sky with beautiful lights and stars and water.

August 15, 1983- I was in another country. This lady told me she was leaving this earth plane in six hours and I was to wear a white blouse.

August 21, 1983- Chippewa Falls. I saw part of a plane that fell to the ground and a hit a silo in a field. No one was hurt.

August 28, 1983- I was in a church. This priest gave me five dollars to light five candles. Then a group of us turned around and sang Silent Night. One lady had a beautiful voice.

September 3, 1984- I dreamt if a man doing martial arts. All he said was two words, Bruce Lee.

September 5, 1984- I could will animals so you could see them. I told someone to look at them and the animals would be gone. It was a lion and a tiger.

September 9, 1984- I was looking at a lady who passed away lying in a coffin. She got up and walked away with her husband.

September 11, 1984- I dreamt of my husband and his family in the spirit world, smiling. His brother's son died.

September 12, 1984- I dreamt of my friends' sister who wanted me to come to the spirit world. I told her no, not yet.

September 15, 1984- Elvis, I was with Elvis Presley when we were standing and talking. He was at peace. He had something in his hand and gave it away.

September 19, 1988- I was sitting by a swimming pool and all of a sudden I started floating across the pool. I did it two times. One woman said it was impossible.

September 21, 1988- Peace, I was playing a song on the tape recorder and I saw the sun and clouds over me. Then I saw the sky light up. The water became very high. It has to be in the East.

October 12, 1989- I dreamt I was in a car accident and saw people from another planet. Then I met this woman from another planet who spoke another language. But I could understand her. It was a very easy language and very beautiful surroundings.

October 18, 1989- I was to meditate on prosperity. Then I was told every thousand years this was the day to ask for anything. Then the year before 4-25-1987 I was told the same thing

October 25, 1989- This man was doing surgery on this other man. His eyes were large and green, hypnotizing him. There was a lot of blood and when it was over, the blood stopped and was gone. He said everything was ok.

November 5, 1989- I dreamt of Hitler and his wife.

December 10, 1990- Healing, meditating on the color red and getting rid of a gland-etc. Then it changed to blue.

December 15, 1990- My death. I could not get a full breath. It took a long time and it was very short. That was the end of that life. I felt peace within me, no fear.

December 21, 1990- An Astrologer woman in my dream said don't cry. Read the stars and I would be changing planes or trains.

December 25, 1990- There was a man named Ramatlia who for told the future. I was in France. This woman told me to take a deep breath. I said I want to see Ramatlia. All of a sudden he appeared with a gold and black crown.

December 30, 1990- I needed more proof with a gust of wind I almost fell over. I know it was Ramatlia. I looked out the window and saw trucks falling over but I knew no one was hurt. I guess he was trying to prove to me who he was. I made a sign of the cross before Ramatlia was just a person.

January 10, 1991- I saw Ghandi in my dream.

January 18, 1991- My dad's sister came to me, touched my hand and said good things will come to me.

January 21, 1991- My friend's husband came to me in this dream. He re-enacted my daughter's death.

January 27, 1991- My mom was in a nursing home and my sister who passed away said the lady running the home was at fault. My mom almost died. Then my sister was in a white dress and looked pure. She was with a little boy at her side.

January 29, 1991- My stepsons' daughter would have problems with her first child. I called my stepson and he said she had trouble with the baby.

February 10, 1991- I saw a beautiful card with a ribbon on it. All it said on the card was Little One. When I first started to work for my husband in the restaurant business he always forgot my name so he called me Little One.

February 13, 1991- My sister called to tell me Beaver, a boy I used to go out with, dies. She said he committed suicide. About three weeks later he came to me in a dream. He was very beautiful with a white and blue light around him. He said someone has a gun to his head, but what he meant was the job he had was putting him under a lot of pressure. Three months later he came back to me in a dream and said everything is ok.

February 20, 1991- I saw God in a dream. He was sitting with his back to me, and turned a little to the right side; and Jesus Christ was standing next to me.

I have written a lot of my dreams down in the past because I feel they are all there for a reason. It may be a good way to keep in touch with our loved ones or to know if there is any trouble we might be able to see it before it really happens.

CHAPTER 11
Poems

Before my moms' energy ran out, she said she saw a river and I asked her if it was beautiful. She said yes. She said no little girls have to float, that she was building a ship and did not know which way to go. She said she put 4 crows on the north, south, east and west so she would know. She talked about her loved ones, I said, did you see Grandma, my moms' mother. She said no, but she saw Uncle Joe,, her mother's brother and said she never knew her Grandma. She said Uncle Joe was sitting on a chair in her room with her. She said he left but would be back. My mother was so full of beauty and love.

While we were talking she started to talk to her loved ones in the spirit world. I asked her if she was ready to go home to God, she said, NO! She said when I do I'm going to heaven. I asked her again about going home and she said yes. I told her I loved her and thank you. She replied thank you for everything. Five days later, right before she left this earth planet she was deleting everything from the time she was born until she was ready to leave. You could hear bits and pieces of what she said but more like mumbling the words for a day and a half. One time she told my sister she was going to practice leaving and coming back. I asked her if she was ready to leave, this time she said yes. She passed on.

I stayed overnight and the next morning when the nurse told me she took her last breath I stood up. This energy came over me and I had a wart on the bottom of my foot, three doctors tried to get rid of it and it never went away. That morning I looked at my foot and it was gone. All this time I felt like I was hanging onto something and it must have been my mom. My parents were the best in this world, very loving and understanding.

My mom wrote poems, I got a letter in the mail one day for a poem writing contest. I told my mom she should write something, she said I should and I told her I'm not a good speller and that she wrote for a T.V station and other people. I put the contest paper away and I thought maybe I'll try to write something. Three months went by and for some reason came across the letter again so I asked my mom if she wrote a poem and she said no. I asked god to help me and I wrote a poem and sent it in. I received a letter saying it took the editors award. My mother could not believe it. So I started writing poems for a while and asked God again to change my life.

"Sketches of the Soul"

This is the poem for my Mother, other Mothers troubles and Mother Earth, as today Mother Earth is in trouble, Mother is a symbol of the heart. An eternal living love, she has nurtured mankind since the beginning of time. Our effort today can save our tomorrow. Let us peacefully celebrate. Happy Mother's Day!

"Mother's Day"

Love is more than poetry or more than words can say.

I see the grace that's in her eyes, she means everything to me.

Every good thing she has given me so please
dear lord what can I give thee.

So please accept this heart of mine that I offer thee.

Even if I see a tear I know it's not fear.

She is so kind and gentle so I give her my love throughout the year.

I see the sun and moon and stars and every flower fair.

I see her gentle grace and love that always fills the air.

When it comes to my Mother she is all of the above and rare.

I see her grace and beauty so what more can
I say, when it comes to Moms',

Happy Mother's Day

A mother's love is closest to Gods' love.

"Poems from the heart with love"

We are love and peace becomes the way for you and me.

We exist at this moment of reflection of who we are.

We are unchanging impartial love and peace.

"You and me"

Time is changing, time is coming; I see a change
when the plants move and the trumpets sound. Gods'
will on Earth and peace for man will come.

"Hello"

I couldn't let this day go by

Without calling, just to say hi.

"Let there be light"

I saw the clouds dark and gray.

I see the lightning strike.

I hear the rolling thunder, and then it starts to rain.

The dark turned into night.

The morning came, the sun came out and God said let there be light.

"I hear you"

I heard you calling, your voice was loud and clear,

when I turned around you were never there.

Love is powerful, love is not just a word or how it comes across.

It's how you use it.

Love is the best teacher.

That's why they call it love.

It is God's love that loves man, not man's love.

"My memory"

There is nothing wrong with my memory.

Its just that you let other thoughts get in the way.

We should live righteously, divinely, in grace with
dignity so we can fine inner peace.

Laugh, this is the purpose of life.

Shine and lift burdens that will go away.

Just forgive and do your best.

Life is a lease on life and space.

Secure your tomorrow, it's time for nations
to come together and greet god.

"My soul"

God made me special, that I know.

It came from above.

He loves me more than I'll ever know.

My Father's thoughts have touched my soul.

"Today"

Today and every day were made for you and me.
You have to power within in you to be what you want to be.

"My Mother"

My Mother always told me when I was growing up to always
read the Good Book and I would find the one I love.

When I sit and meditate I always pray to God that he
is always listening and can read my thoughts.

"My Mom"

My mother used to dress me and that's the way I would stay.
I always looked so funny.
And now I dress that way.

"For you"

I love you very much for all that you have done for me.
Now you are with God and Mom is still with me.
Happy Father's Day

"My Sister"

I looked up at my sister as she was looking down at me.
She was asking, what I was doing?
I said writing poetry.

"Everything comes to pass"

Now the floods are gone.
It makes you want to think.
Only keep what you need and always keep the faith.

"Reflections"

I see the love that fills the air in every face I see.
When I look at someone else, it's a reflection of me.

"Dancing in the sun"

The sun shines on the water,
It dances with delight;
It dances on the water in the dark moonlight.

"Freedom"

I see the sunlight through the trees.
I feel nature's gentle breeze.
God made this universe for you and me.
God gave us the freedom to be free.

"See yourself"

My Father is coming through me.
With all these beautiful thoughts.
He is telling man to see himself as God.
Or this world will be lost.

"**Future**"

I see the future where no man has ever been.
I sit here waiting and praying God will take my hand.

"**I am free**"

Today I am thirty.
Today I am free to thank myself for being me.

"**Loving you**"

Everything I say and everything I do doesn't come from a book.
It comes from loving you.

"**Laughter**"

Having success and prosperity and having a wonderful life;
will always bring laughter into my life.

"**Stars**"

The stars are not just diamonds in the sky.
They are full of love and dance with joy.
They twinkle; they're bright and big.
Now I know this world is big.

"**Angles**"

Angles don't have wings like butterflies and birds,
But are God's thoughts coming to us to fill out hearts with cheer.

"**Visualize**"

Close your eyes and visualize where you want to be.
Open your eyes and keep those thoughts and you will be set free.

"I Know You Love Me"

I'm with you always. Yes I love you. You are there, I'm here.
I feel your love that's in the air. We have the freedom to be free.
We're to free spirits God set free to come and go whenever we please.
My love for you is very deep to have the courage to complete.
My love for you is everywhere that fills the sky above.
I see the love that's in your eyes. Some day we will be one.
I can't conceal in my eyes the love for you that never dies.
My love for you is everywhere. My love for you I'll always share.
God gave me this love to give to you. My love for you I cannot bear.
My love for you will always be for now throughout eternity.
Our path in life is free.

"My Dream"

I saw him coming in a dream. He is near, walking toward me,
His clothes flowing and the light around him
glowing. He kept coming toward me
He disappeared the thoughts I have of him. He will soon be here.

"You are Beautiful"

You are beautiful. All your life you did for others.
Sometimes there was despair, but in your heart you knew better.
The love for others was always there.

"Birth"

Life isn't that bad so don't complain. You took birth on this earth plane.
Live it out or you will come back to live again and again.

"Smile"

When I look at life, what do I see?
I see God filling every space with love that keeps surrounding me.
I smile back at God and he smiles back at me.

"Nature Turning"

The trees are turning, the birds are chirping.
Mother Nature's flowers are turning.
The winds are coming, the skies are changing.
To let us know that winter is coming.

"Thoughts"

I thought one day what life would be. I saw all the signs pointing at me.
As love flows from every heart, I see its time to do my part.
Now is the time to let peace flow from every heart.
Every good thing comes from above.

Every good thing comes from God.

It's time for peace, it's time for joy.

God only made good, so there is no time to cry.

"Shadows"

When you walk on the path of life and see the shadows
of light with every step along the way, bestows the
grace that can turn this world your way.

"Only God"

Only god can make your dreams come true.

Only God can make the waters blue.

Only God can turn the night to day.

Only God can keep you safe each day.

Only God can free you from a fall.

Only God can make the heavens above and fill every space with love.

Only God can hold your hand.

Only God can understand.

"Treasures"

Only what we can fulfill and walk in the right direction.

When we look at where out treasures are and where our hearts are going.

"My Purpose in Life"

I am full of grace, peace and love that always come my way.

The purpose of being and know my purpose is here.

"Grace"

The love and air we breathe is a fragrance that comes from above.
God unites us with his love.
It gives us growth in grace and patience every day.
God gives us meekness, joy and illuminates our way.

"Autumn"

I see a change from spring to autumn.
The leaves are falling with every breath I take.
The butterflies are leaving with their gentle grace.
They will be back next year to bloom and fly in the air.

"Count Your Blessings"

Did you count your blessings and know that they were true?
Did you find peace in your heart?
Did your keep the faith and say I love you?

"Be Mine"

I am just a soul in love with you.
So will you be mine and always be my valentine?

"Two Birthdays"

I only have two birthdays to celebrate.
The time I was born and when I die.

"A Cause"

Everyone is fighting for a cause.
The only cause should be God.

"Winter"

It started to rain, then started to freeze and left the ice on the trees.
The sun reflected on the ice.
It was possible Jack Frost was out for the night.

"I Can't Sleep"

When I went to bed and could not sleep.
I started counting Gods name instead of sheep.

"Plant a Seed"

Plant a seed and watch it grow.
You can become as strong as a tree and everything else will unfold.

"Reflections of Life"

God is love and we reflect that love.

The clouds above me, the earth beneath my feet.

The air that surrounds me, the beauty within me.

"Courage"

God gave us the courage to confess the wrong that
we have done, or harm and hurt to anyone.

Give us the strength and courage to be free and
love others as you would love me.

"Good Morning"

When you wake up this morning did you do what you had to do?

Did you love on another and make sure you knew the truth?

Did you look at someone else and feel the way they do?

"Nature"

When I think of nature, this is what I see:

I see the birds that build their nests as the deer run through the trees.

I see the chipmunks run around and feed their hungry cheeks.

I see the sunlight through the trees. I feel nature's gentle breeze.

God made this universe for you and me, God
gave us the freedom to be free.

"Heaven"

Heaven is not in the sky or beyond the sea.
Heaven is right here with you and me.

"Keep the Courage"

If you should falter and be discouraged take
up the cross and keep the courage.

"Obstacles"

If obstacles get in your way, only let go to know that God is really near.
Be filled with light. Be filled with the His love will cast out all your fears.

"To Hear You"

It's always nice to hear your voice for what you have to say
Your words are sweet and full of love that makes a perfect day.

"Look at Me"

Look at me. What do you see? I only see the good in you and me.

"Timeless"

Age is timeless and you are great.
O As you grow in grace you will see God face to face.
So think of God's name with every breath you take.
God watches over us. Until we leave this world so we can all be free.

There will be light, love and peace. No more
tears. No more fears. No more doubt.

He will whisper in our ear, I love you.

God will set us free from a world of delusion that can never harm me.

Open your heart and let the love pour out for all the world to see.

"Light"

Be filled with light. Be filled with the light
as we are the light of the world.

"Wake Up"

When we wake up we will see the world is only a dream.

"Peace"

Love an peace becomes the way as false beliefs
dissolve for all the human race.

"Space"

We are love. We exist at this moment.

Now we are a reflection of what we see.

As love pours from the heart, we are impartial love of peace.

"Health"

Fashion every flower. Fashion every weed.

Death is more beautiful than the human eye can see.

"I Saw Him Coming"

I saw him coming. I saw him in a dream.
Walking toward me his clothes were flowing
the light around him glowing.

"My Mom"

I know my Mom is with me. I feel her presence each day.
I believe she is telling me to go on with my life,
to know what she went through and to guide me with her life.
The day will come when she can rest to know I did my best.

"Don't Lose Faith"

It is not an act of God; it is an act of man.
When things get dark and dreary and you start to lose your faith,
cling to God and will restore your faith.

"Angles of Love"

Angles all surrounding us, they are with us every day.
To fill our hearts with peace, love and joy to help in every way.

"Forgive"

This is the time for forgiveness. We are the light of the world.
All it takes you and me to see this world is free.
God made the hills and sandy roads for us to walk upon.
We must respect the things God made or soon it will be gone.
I see the future where man has never been.

My father is coming through me with all these beautiful thoughts.

He is telling man to see himself, as God, or this world will be lost.

"Sister Dear"

Sister dear I love you. You left this world without a tear.

You gave me so much. Now you're gone. Your love fir life will carry on.

You opened your eyes of blue to see one more time.

You took two breathes and left.

With grace, love and dignity God gave you his grace, love and might.

Now you are in the light.

I see your face as it shines. You will come again one more time.

"Edgar Cayce"

God made us special that I know.

It came from up above.

He loves us more than we will ever know.

My father's thoughts have touched my soul.

"Aquarius"

The Age of Aquarius is coming our way we have to take away emptiness,

insanity and pain for judgment day.

We sit in the world, we have to remain
disciplined in this undisciplined world.

We have to master ourselves. We need character, commitment and grace.

We have to overflow with energy, touch their
hearts and fill their empty space.

Our actions will be great. We will create a new humanity.

Create the Age of Aquarius for the human race, and fill every space.

We want life to be right for our children for the
whole society to find inner peace.

To laugh and love and shine cause life is only a lease on time and space.

Do your part and live in peace

This world would disappear from view; it would always be the same.

CHAPTER 12
CREATE A POSITIVE LIFE

Wake up to your own inner courage.

When you wake in the morning and throughout the day repeat some saying to keep you uplifted. Transform your thoughts and life completely. Think well of yourself and others. God has given us the sword of reason which we can use to free ourselves from this world of delusion. That God-given power of discrimination to choose right action in preference to wrong action; to be mentally above your troubles. Just know and believe in your heart. Think of God planting love in your heart day and night. Use your own spiritual effort so you can remove the veil of ignorance from your consciousness.

Honor yourself.

Respect yourself.

Meditate upon yourself.

Kneel to yourself as God dwells within you. Surrender yourself with the protective force of love, peace and harmony. Resolve, eliminate and repel negative influences from any source. Think of a powerful brilliant aura that repels negativity. Enhance your natural ability to receive psychic impressions, insights and information about yourself and others.

Know psychic impressions come to me easily. I am a natural channel of universal insights and wisdom. I am more psychic every day. I have powerful psychic ability. Man walks in the direction where he looks, where his treasures are, where his heart is.

Everything spiritual comes from above. Know the truth about yourself and all your actions will bear fruit. When you get good thoughts those are angel thoughts passing from God to man. Don't go through life with blinders on. Don't put weight on your heart. Relax or it will make the situation worse. However things go you must remain calm, quiet and peaceful. That peace is the source of prosperity. Self –containment is the act of prosperity and it is the highest spiritual strength. There is nothing greater.

Smile

There is an ocean of love within all of us. The love of God is so pure. It is unconditional. It is always there if you allow yourself to drink this love. Even if you make the simple effort you can experience this love. Allow this understanding to take you higher and higher. Make it more and more divine.

Trust Yourself

Believe in which is not, in order that it may be the imaginations he created power in our hands. Everything in which we have faith succeeds, just as miracles happen through slow motion exercises.

Give all your problems to god.

God will guide you moment my moment.

Be grateful for your knowledge.

O sun let my lost strength be restored.

We are aware of the universe.

We are on a journey going through a planetary shift. You can meditate to help those who are suffering. Think of them in your prayers. If you have a sick mind it will cause sick organs, you will suffer, only think well of people or they will not heal. Always be grateful for the beauty around you. Poor indeed is he who does not show anger, but worse indeed is he who cannot control it in himself and there must fail.

Wake up to Your Own Courage

Very often those who flare up quickly also forgive quickly. Remain as a little child asking, seeking, and living. Guide me O God in the steps I take, in the words I say day by day. By letting go all gets done. The world is won by those who let go. When you try and try, it is even be on winning, I think of this world as a beautiful garden and everyone in it a flower. Inner wealth is called the heart. Surrender to one's own self. The greater the self the higher the self, wrap your problems in a bundle and give to God. Turn within the force behind your actions and thoughts with faith. You become free in the world.

When you do good that good comes from the good within. Don't doubt. Magnetize it. Let it come to you. Right is right, wrong is wrong. If you want to criticize someone look in the mirror. Thank yourself.

Create a Positive Life

In the beginning God created the heavens and earth, and then there was light. Now is the time of the new beginning a new dawn. As God, will of God is expressed on earth with understanding of light, love and peace. We should all do our part. God dwells in you as you for God is all in all.

Open up your heart and let the pure presence of unconditional love pour out. Know you are with the light, filled with the light, illumined by its light. You are the light of the world. Send forth the light, merge with the light. We are the light of the world. There is one light of love, peace and understanding. Its moving across the face of the Earth, touching and illuminating every soul. All kingdoms of the Earth will respond. The planet will be alive with light, love, peace and understanding. A new dawn is moving across the face of the Earth, touching and illuminating every soul.

With total oneness let love flow from every heart. Forgiveness begins in every soul. Now the light of the world there is once presence and power of the universe. God is healing and harmonizing planet Earth. Create inner peace. Listen to music. Think of gentle winds, tropical oceans. They are challenges to our creativity if you want an abundance of fortuitous opportunities into your life. I feel lucky today. I have incredibly good luck. My positive dreams are becoming my reality. I attract harmony and good luck. There is a steady flow of good luck in my life. Everything in the past dies yesterday; everything in the future was born today. The greatest enemy of the self is if you do not respect the self.

Control time; do not let it control you. Set objectives and establish priorities to create extra hours in the day. Be enthusiastic, set daily goals. Feel great satisfaction when you accomplish your goals. Stay on course and reach your goals. This is also good for children too. Look at God in everything. Know you are a self-starter and enjoy getting things done. Look at the good in people. Set your affections on the things above. Not on Earth or who we are, but the expression of unchanging love and divine wisdom.

Be a free thinker. Release the flow of creative ideas in your mind. Know you have a great creative genie within you. Angels are God's thoughts passing to man. When you get an angel thought nurture your creativity into expression. Do not lack ideas. Know you are filled with inspiration. Whatever is possible to God is possible for you to accomplish with God's help. Stand your ground with truth and love and you will win. God's will is that you remain free. Be a free thinker. Forgive yourself and your past. Remove the veil of ignorance from your consciousness,

Keep your thoughts free from thinking about illness. Know that all your channels are filled with truth and love. If you have a problem or pain, zap it out right away. If you cater to your children you will lose them. If you do not pass down your values you expand the ego to such an extent that there is nothing to stop it. Their life becomes destructive and then the child will disobey parents and leave the home.

Just accept the wrong and try to do it right. Don't believe that wrong has to be punished, or to lock up a person or kill himself. Everyday say to yourself, "I shall live this day with grace". If you keep complaining about your job and environment it will bring misery. Compliments bring strength. It is our birthright to be happy but it you do not practice discipline you will never be happy.

By meditating we take our inner self garbage out. When you have spiritual powers you shine like the sun. People have more faith in the material things than the spiritual because they have separated themselves from God. If you let the senses control you your senses will take over and win. When your health becomes bad change your negative thoughts into positive right away. Don't exchange one disease for another. All addictions come from the same source, promising satisfaction. We are children of God and sometimes we get off track. Putting stress and limitations on yourself stops the flow of circulation just as anxiety. It will cause the body illness and diseases. Don't hang on your problems or they will just get bigger and bigger. Drop the problems right away.

Have faith and trust in God and he will take care of it in his own way, and his own time. The mind is very powerful. If you can think it you can do it. Sometimes you give people the power to hurt you. Change your negative thoughts into positive right away before the problem gets out of hand. Then you yourself can't handle it. You picked this life and you have to live it out or your lesson will just get tougher.

If you have odds with someone, bless then. Share your love and send your love to them. In a few days you will feel better. Don't have idols. You will lose your true identity of who you really are. Be careful who you pick for your friends. They reflect you and you reflect them. Breathe in just for today. Just for today let go of the anger and worry. Count your blessings. Live honestly and be kind to all living things. If you want to judge others, judge yourself first. Those who are grateful always become great, full of wealth and prosperous. May this be our path. You are the light of the world.

It isn't what goes into the mouth; it's what comes out of the mouth that matters. If you have a stirring within you listen to God for his ideas. Be filled with God's inspiration and express it in a creative wa. Fill yourself with healing, love and energy. Adapt to life changes. All things will work together for the glory of God.

Work out your own salvation. Free yourself of guilt or blaming yourself or others. Enjoy a new life with love, kindness and acceptance. Forgive and release yourself of all guilt. Welcome and express a sense of peace and tranquility about yourself. Keep positive, loving thoughts and memories. Start each day with a clean slate.

Do something positive with your life. Snap out of the way you feel. Repeat: I have tremendous willpower and I can accomplish anything I set my mind to. I am a powerhouse of determination. My mind is made up. Nothing can deter me. I have a strong determination to succeed.

Release the knowledge in your subconscious that you have a strong and powerful memory. Know it is easy to remember desired information. You have complete confidence in your ability that your memories will rise effortlessly to the surface. With your imagination don't let your energy go backwards. Go forward and change evil thoughts to spiritual. Have faith. Whatever happens remain in control, tranquil and serene, regardless of the circumstances. Be a patient person. Grow more patience and understanding every day. Let it surround you. Be relaxed, calm and at ease. Automatically become calm under stress. Let fears and worry dissolve from your life. Radiate faith, belief and confidence into yourself. Today know you are free of fear and worry. Replace negative thoughts with positive ones. Know you are confident and secure.

In the new dawn you will see the salvation of the planet before your eyes. Separation is no more. The healing has taken place. The world is restored to sanity. This will be the beginning of peace on Earth good will toward all. Let love flow from every heart, forgiveness in every soul, all hearts and minds will be one in perfect understanding. Unity will be achieved. Oneness we rein in every heart.

All the creative power of Gods Universe is within you. If you cant heal yourself, you cannot heal anybody. You have to become a student before you become a teacher.

CHAPTER 13
The Author

May this book bless you every day, God is the real author. God is in control. Gayle is a self –realized spiritual person. She has a strong bond with herself. She looks at life with light and love through her eyes. She has dedicated her life to God and to others. She says you are nothing less than light an d love. She taught herself in many ways.

Gayle is a Yoga instructor of 45 years, volunteers at many places. She has received special commendation awards in recognition of significant contributions to community life in Wisconsin as well as being and activist for 20 years in her community. She has been on national television for another book that she has written, and donated it to the Edgar Cayce A.R.E. clinic foundation and the library.

She had the best parents in the world. She is an activist in her community and does public relations. She has many poems and one took the Editors Award. She would like to write a book on Yoga and has written a true story based on 'Joseph and the Amazing Technicolor Dream Coat". It is about love and forgiveness. She was hoping that her friend would do a movie on it, like the deep blue sea, and her friend's song would be a number one hit for her story.

She is a volunteer to the Veterans; her friend was in the Vietnam War. He wrote a beautiful song that touches the heart called, "So Far From Home". After reading an article I read what Phil Donahue wrote, this song goes out to all the vets who served their country.

A Woman of Strength

A strong woman works out every day to keep her body in shape . . . but a woman of strength kneels in prayer to keep her soul in shape . . .

A strong woman isn't afraid of anything . . . but a woman of strength shows courage in the midst of her fear . . .

A strong woman won't let anyone get the best of her . . . but a woman of strength gives the best of herself to everyone . . .

A strong woman makes mistakes and avoids the same in the future . . . a woman of strength realizes life's mistakes can also be blessings and capitalizes on them . . .

A strong woman walks sure footedly . . . but a woman of strength knows God will catch her when she falls . . .

A strong woman wears the look of confidence on her face . . . but a woman of strength wears grace . . .

A strong woman has faith that she is strong enough for the journey . . . but a woman of strength has faith that it is in the journey that she will become strong.

—Anonymous

Before you end the day do something for yourself. You are special. Always whisper in your child's ear each night that whatever they need will come to them. Always be one with God on your lips until your last breathe that he would have the connection to do it. Pray for your children. Think of them having a radiant body and they will get energy from it. Whisper to them when they go to bed to become one with God so no matter what challenges he faces he would have the connection to carry him through it.

Let nothing upset you. Everything is changing, God alone is changeless. Patience attains the good. Who has God lacks nothing. God alone fills our needs.

Thank you for reading this book. I hope it will help you to lead a more powerful exciting life. Remember you can heal yourself in the Aquarian age. Self-healing is the process of relationship between the infinite power of the soul. It is from a state of compassion meditation, that the healing activity if God within the being flows. We are nothing without God. Never underestimate the power of God.

Thoughts become feelings, then they become emotions, then that becomes desires, then that becomes. The mistakes you make occur because you are attached to your emotions and you lose your good judgment. Let your ego go. When selfishness and conceit go away, peace comes and the mind and body are healed. Then you will forgive and be healthy. O mind think well of yourself and others. After reading this book I hope it will change our left and get back on track for judgment day; A new beginning a new dawn the final chapter.

Remembering the one God in meditation, all diseases are healed. Only constant remembering of your true identity brings true health.

I will always think of Edgar Cayce as a great being and this world an ocean of joy. Stay on a spiritual path, change your beliefs now. Forgive the past. Wake up and your will see the world is only an illusion, only a dream. "All my thoughts come from God". May God bless America, may God bless this world, let us sing God Bless America.

Namaste

From my heart to your heart with great respect and love.

Gayle

Sunday Aug 19, 2012 4:30 AM

I was standing on this land. I saw a river in front of me I did not know the name.

I heard a voice say the "JORDAN". This must be the place we will see God.

"A New Beginning a New Dawn"

This book is based on the author's knowledge and experiences. What she had with God, herself and others. It is about changing your life. As you can heal yourself through prayers, and having a positive attitude and to laugh more to show the world you can do it for yourself. You are the one that counts. Heal yourself with forgiveness; see people with the spiritual eye not the physical eye. Don't lower yourself to any ones level as you reflect your friends and they reflect you. If you can't change your life you will take it with you. Stay on a spiritual path, pour peace and love into yourself. Win the grace of your mind, keep it calm and serene. Have more grace than space. Fill yourself with peace and love if you have the strength within you. Nurture your creativity into expression, know your outfield with inspiration and can express it best in creative ways. Don't worship your problems. Having a fixed mind you will always have problems. Wrap your problems in a bundle and give them to God. Fill yourself with good, gratitude, joy, warmth and good thoughts. There is no space for anger, fear, criticism or illness. Know the truth and the truth will set you free.